John Scot

The Staggering State of Scottish Statesmen from 1550 to 1650

With a memoir of the author and historical illustrations

John Scot

The Staggering State of Scottish Statesmen from 1550 to 1650
With a memoir of the author and historical illustrations

ISBN/EAN: 9783337243913

Printed in Europe, USA, Canada, Australia, Japan

Cover: Foto ©ninafisch / pixelio.de

More available books at **www.hansebooks.com**

THE STAGGERING STATE

OF

SCOTTISH STATESMEN

From 1550 to 1650

By SIR JOHN SCOT of Scotstarvet,

WITH

A Memoir of the Author and Historical Illustrations

BY THE

Rev. CHARLES ROGERS, LL.D., F.S.A. Scot.

Historiographer to the Historical Society.

EDINBURGH:
WILLIAM PATERSON, PRINCES STREET.

1872.

[ONE HUNDRED COPIES.]

PREFACE.

The "Staggering State" has been reprinted, neither on account of its historical value, nor in evidence of the capacity or learning of its author. It is a work unique of its kind—a performance in which biographical details are blended with that peculiar gossip which is the offspring of envy and all uncharitableness. It is a record of history and calumny—a repository of fireside chit-chat respecting conspicuous persons at a period when, if, on the one hand, statesmen served themselves rather than the State, on the other, evil report proved an intellectual relish to many who were capable of more rational enjoyments. In connexion with the performance, it is not the least remarkable feature that it was composed by one who frequented the first circles, was related to the best families, and was one of the most learned persons in the kingdom. Nay, more, the author was in some matters singularly generous; his benefactions were munificent, and his patriotism equalled his benevolence. Yet he has withal produced a most uncharitable book; and it may be questioned whether Sir Anthony Weldon himself has dealt with Scotsmen after a severer fashion. On the old maxim of the Regent Mar, he has "spoken furth, and spared nocht;" and, like the Scottish Wife of Bath, has given all their *dittay*, or accusal, without pity and without remorse. He has scattered firebrands, and few of his contemporaries have escaped. He wrote while writhing under disappointment and public wrong. Probably he intended to give vent to his resentment, and then to allow what he had written to perish with the angry passion which evoked it. The "Staggering State" was written when the author had reached his eightieth year. Upwards of other fourscore years it remained unprinted—copies, however, being multiplied in MS. Of these many were incorrectly written. In 1754 Walter Goodal prevailed on the firm of Walter Ruddiman and Co. to print an edition which he had prepared; this work, in a duodecimo of 190 pages, has latterly become scarce. Mr. Goodal edited carefully; he founded his text on an old MS. which he believed to be contemporaneous, and to contain "additions, and even whole lives, in the author's own hand." That MS. is preserved in the Advocates Library (press-mark, 34, 3, 2), and while its contemporaneity may be doubted, it is unquestionably ancient. Of two other MSS. in the Advocates Library, one, a thin folio (press-mark, 34, 3, 1) seems to belong to a date anterior to the MS. used by Goodal. The other is modern. Two MSS., one in the Library of the British Museum, and the other in the University Library, St. Andrews, are of no particular value. Two others, one belonging to the close of the seventeenth, and the other to the beginning of the eighteenth century, have been placed at the editor's disposal by Mr. Laing of Edinburgh.

After a careful examination of the various MSS., the editor has not felt justified in making any material alteration on the text arranged by Goodal. That Goodal has modernized the author's orthography may not be overmuch censured, for each transcriber seems to have adopted his own mode of spelling, and when the present editor attempted to restore the original reading, he encountered difficulties which were insuperable. Some of Goodal's notes have been retained; also his "Account of the Great Officers of State," and his "List" of these Officers from the earliest times till the Restoration. For his "List" Goodal has acknowledged his obligations to the collections of Sir James Balfour and Dr. George Mackenzie.

The Memoir of Sir John Scot has, as a whole, been prepared from original sources of information. The details of his life cause a regret that his name should be associated with the gossip of "The Staggering State." He was one of the most enterprising Scotsmen of his age—he exercised an independent judgment on all questions ecclesiastical and civil; and though desirous of retaining the emoluments of office, he devoted a portion of his wealth to the interests of the State and the welfare of his countrymen. In his old age, writhing under disappointment, he dipped his pen in gall and smote everywhere. Happily, from the universality of his attacks, none have suffered materially. It would be ridiculous that any descended from the sufferers should now utter a complaint. Better is it to reflect that we live in times when men differ on public topics without cherishing mutual hate, and when calumny more frequently recoils upon the utterer than reaches its victim.

The editor regrets that the Earl of Morton has had no leisure to furnish copies of several of the author's letters preserved in his Lordship's repositories. The readiness of the Duke of Portland to furnish information has been creditable to his Grace, both as Sir John Scot's representative and as a member of the Peerage. To Mr. David Laing, Mr. M. F. Conolly, and others who have rendered most essential assistance, the editor's best acknowledgments are due.

SNOWDOUN VILLA, LEWISHAM, S.E.
Feb., 1872.

MEMOIR.

SIR JOHN SCOT was descended from the House of Buccleuch; by using a single "t" he preserved the original orthography of his family name. His progenitor, David Scot of Allanhaugh, represented the eleventh generation of the Scots of Buccleuch in the direct male line. David Scot of Allanhaugh obtained a charter of the lands of Whitchester in 1483; he died about 1530, leaving three sons, Robert, Alexander, and James. James, the youngest, entered the Church, and became Provost of Corstorphine. A man of high integrity and honour, he gave proof of his generosity by erecting a manse at Corstorphine for the use of his successors. He was elected Clerk to the Treasury, and an ordinary Lord of Session on the spiritual side of that court. He died in 1563.* Sir Alexander, second son of David Scot, was in 1534 appointed Vice-Register of Scotland. He died in 1540. His eldest son, Robert, studied law, acquired eminence in his profession, and was chosen a Clerk of Session. As eldest Clerk of Session he was, on the death of James Macgill in 1579, entitled to succeed him as Clerk Register. He declined the appointment, which was accepted by Alexander Hay, Clerk of the Privy Council, who in Scot's favour afterwards resigned the directorship of the Chancery.†

Robert Scot was appointed Clerk of Parliament and Director of the Chancery by a writ under the great seal, dated 17th October, 1579. He acquired the lands of Knightspottie in Perthshire, and married, first, Elizabeth Sandilands, a daughter of the house of Calder, who died without surviving issue; and secondly, Elizabeth, widow of John Scott, of Orchardfield, maltman, West Port, Edinburgh, and mother by her first husband of Sir William Scott of Ardross, Fifeshire.‡ By this marriage Robert Scot became father of two sons and a daughter. The

* Brunton and Haig's "Senators of the College of Justice," 99.
† "Staggering State" under "Directors of Chancery."
‡ "Inquisitiones Speciales," II. (1554.)

daughter married James, only son and heir of Andrew Hop-Pringle, of Smailholm, and Galashiels.* James, the younger son, was styled of Vogrie. Robert, the eldest, received the directorship of the Chancery on the resignation of his father in 1582; but being in feeble health he resigned the office, in which his father was reinstated. He died in 1588. By his marriage with Margaret, daughter of Alexander Aitcheson, of Gosford, Haddingtonshire (ancestor of the Earls of Gosford), he was father of one son—the subject of this Memoir.

To secure his grandson in the Chancery directorship, Robert Scot of Knightspottie demitted the office, in 1592, to William Scott of Ardross, his wife's second son; receiving from him a bond that he would on the coming of age of the infant John Scot, vacate the post in his favour. Robert Scot died on the 28th March, 1592.†

John Scot was born in 1586. He entered St. Leonard's College, St. Andrews. In the register of that college he subscribes himself, in 1603, "Johannes Scot cursus sui anno tertio." He matriculated on the 20th December, 1602. From St. Andrews he proceeded to one of the continental universities, for the study of classical learning. He was admitted advocate about 1606, and in that year, on the resignation of William Scott of Ardross, he obtained the directorship of the Chancery held by three generations of his house.‡ On the 25th October, 1611, he received a charter to the lands of Overtown, Nethertown, and East Caiplie in Fife; and on the 28th November of the same year, a charter to the lands of Tarvet in the same county. To the latter he prefixed his own family name, and was henceforth known as Scot of Scotstarvet.§ In 1617 he was sworn a member of the Privy Council, and knighted by James VI. He evinced his gratitude by composing a long Latin poem in celebration of the

---

* Douglas Baronage, 221-4.

† Robert Scot is by the poet Alexander Montgomery celebrated in the following epitaph:—

"Good Robert Scot, sen thou art gone to God,
 Cheif of our souerane Colledge Justice Clerks,—
Vho, vhill thou liv'd, for honestie wes od
 As wryt beris witness of thy worthy werks:
So faithful, formall, and so frank and frie
Sall nevir vse that office eftir thee."

Montgomery's Poems, edited by David Irving, Edin., 1821, 8vo., p. 243.

‡ Staggering State.   § Douglas Baronage, 222.

royal visit. It is printed in a tract of forty pages, entitled, " Hodœporicon in serenissimi et invictissimi Principis Jacobi Sexti é Scotia sua decessum," Edin., 1619, 4to.

On the accession of Charles I. Sir John recommended himself to the new monarch. On this subject Sir James Balfour writes:—

"S^r· Johne Scott, Director of the Chancelerey about this same tyme (September, 1626), a bussie man in foule wether, and one quhosse coueteousnesse far exceidit his honesty, did exhibit some artickells to his Matie anent the alteratione of tenurs and haldinges, and the omissione of marriages, wich by the king wes recommendit to S$_r$. Thomas Hope, one of his aduocats, to be put to a trayell, and to prosecut the same to his Maiesties profitt and comodity."[*] Sir John's counsel, thus quaintly described, proved the commencement of that distrust in the king's exercise of the prerogative which ultimately led to his overthrow.

Injudicious as a politician, Sir John was not amenable to the charge of " covetousness ; " he had already proved himself a generous promoter of learning. In 1620 he made a donation of books to the library of St. Leonard's College, St. Andrews, and at the same time granted to the Regents of that institution lands and rents for the endowment of a Professorship of Humanity or Latin. To the history of that endowment we will afterwards refer.

Sir John conducted a wide correspondence, chiefly in the Latin tongue, with learned persons both at home and abroad. In the Advocates Library, a folio volume contains numerous letters and Latin verses, addressed to him by his correspondents. On the first page, this volume is inscribed, " Ex dono M^{ri} Davidis Cunynghame studijs Comitis de Carnwath præpositi." The history of the donor is otherwise unknown. Among Sir John's correspondents whose letters are preserved in the volume, we meet with the names of Arthur Johnston, Caspar Barlaeus,[†] and Isaac Gruter, the two latter learned Dutchmen, who have celebrated Sir John in Latin verse. There are

---

[*] Balfour's Annals, ii., 147.

[†] Caspar Barlaeus or Van Baarle, a Dutch Latin poet, was born at Antwerp in 1584. He was some time Professor of Logic in the University of Leyden, and afterwards occupied the Chair of Philosophy and Rhetoric in the Athenæum at Amsterdam. His poems, which are numerous and on a great variety of subjects, were first printed at Leyden in 1631. He published other works, also in the Latin tongue.

also letters from William Barlaeus, Peter Goldman, Antony Clemens, William Janson, John Leech, Edinburgh, and John Bleau, the geographer.

Interested in the volumes of a work commenced in Bleau's printing-house in 1608, containing the best specimens of modern Latin poetry on the Continent,* Sir John resolved to include contemporary Scottish Latin poets in the same series, under the editorship of Arthur Johnston. The undertaking was accomplished in 1637, in two thick duodecimo volumes, with the title, "Delitiæ Poetarvm Scotorvm, hujus ævi Illvstrivm. Amsterdami, apud Iohannem Blaev." While this work was in course of preparation, Sir John visited Amsterdam, and there assisted in correcting the proof-sheets, while he formed the acquaintance of the enterprising printer. That acquaintance led to another undertaking, to be noticed in the sequel. The printing of "The Scots Poets" cost "a hundred double pieces," † or £150 sterling, which Sir John wholly defrayed. In the two volumes of the *Delitiæ*, the poets are arranged alphabetically in the order of their names. By Arthur Johnston the work is inscribed to Sir John Scot, in a flattering prose dedication, which is followed by laudatory verses addressed to him by Johnston, Gruter, and Caspar Barlaeus. Johnston has summoned all the Muses to celebrate his patron. Sir John's own Latin verses are described as excelling those of his contemporaries, as the moon excels the stars; but this judgment posterity has not affirmed. Of his nineteen compositions contained in this work, the most ambitious is the "Hodœporicon," formerly printed. One poem is dated 1603, being composed when the author was a student at St. Leonard's College. His Latinity is fair, but his poetical merits are more than eclipsed by his acts of munificence.

Sir John was appointed an Extraordinary Lord of Session, in January, 1629, an office in which he was succeeded by Sir John Hamilton, in November, 1630. He was nominated an Ordinary Lord of Session on the 28th July, 1632,‡ and took his seat as Lord Scotstarvet. A zealous upholder of royalty, he was nevertheless warmly attached to Presbyterianism, and when Charles I. sought to impose Episcopacy,

---

* The series, which was completed in 1693, extended to twenty volumes, and included compositions of the best Latin poets in Italy, France, Germany, Hungary, Denmark, and the Low Countries.

† "Staggering State," *postea*.　　　　　　‡ Brunton & Haig., 280.

he emphatically protested. He disapproved the introduction of the Service Book in 1637, and on the 30th April of the following year attended at his parish church of Ceres,* and there, with the minister, elders and parishioners, subscribed the Covenant. That document embraced the Confession of Faith of 1580, subscribed by James VI., and which bound all who signed it to defend their religion with their lives. In November, 1638, Sir John renewed his protest against the royal policy by refusing to subscribe " the Confession," or Declaration tendered by the king's Commissioner, and stated his belief that the settlement of religion should be entrusted to the General Assembly. He further affirmed his conviction that the document submitted was not in harmony with the " Confession of King James." In his declinature he was joined by Sir Alexander Gibson (Lord Durie), Sir John Hope (Lord Craighall), and Sir George Erskine, three senators of the court.† It is interesting to find that he was careful to procure an authentic copy of King James's " Confession." That copy is preserved in the Advocates Library, with the following indorsation :—" Covenant subscryved be King James of worthie memorie and his household, 28th Jary. 1580. Sent from Somer, in France, be Monseur [the name illegible] to my Lord Scottistarvett, in August, 1641."

In 1640 Sir John was placed on the Committee of Estates for defence of country ‡ On the 30th July, 1641, he was, along with the Lords Craighall and Durie, ordered to attend the parliament then sitting.§ On the 13th November of that year, when a new commission to the Court of Session was granted, with the sanction of the Estates, he was re-appointed a judge, *ad vitam aut culpam.*|| During the same year he appeared at the bar of the General Assembly, as appellant from a judgment of the Synod of Fife. To the church living of Kilrenny, in Fife, he had secured the appointment of Mr. Mungo Law, one of the ministers of Dysart, and the translation being disapproved by the Presbytery of St. Andrews and the Synod of Fife, he resolved to debate the case in the Assembly. In a letter to his relative, the Rev. William Spang, minister at Campvere, Principal Baillie alludes to the discussion in these words :—

* Kirksession Records of Ceres.
† Balfour's Annals, II., 293-5. ‡ Baillie's Letters and Journals, I., 309.
§ Balfour's Annals, III., 26. || Acts Parl. v., 466.

"Tuesday, the 3rd of August, was taken up with a very captious question of your good friend, Sir John Scot. He had promised to Mr. Mungo Law, second minister at Dysart, in the Presbytery of Kirkcaldy, a presentation to the kirk at Kilrennie, in the Presbytery of St. Andrews. The Presbytery of St. Andrews were not very curious to crave his transportation; Sir John, in the Provincial Synod of Fife, urges it. In the voicing, not only the whole Presbytery of Kirkcaldy gets voices, but some burrow two ruling elders get voices. Upon this, and some other informalities, Sir John appealed to the General Assembly. By strong solicitation and by a world of merry tales in the face of the Assembly, he gets a sentence for his appellation, to the great indignation of the Synod of Fife, and the Moderator's malcontentment. Sir John held him with that advantage, and durst not pursue his main point, anent the minister's transportation, which made many take him for a wrangler, who sought more the Synod's disgrace than other contentment."*

Mr. Law, Sir John's *protégé*, remained at Dysart till 1644, when he was translated to Greyfriars' Church, Edinburgh.†

With a real and substantial grievance Sir John appeared some years afterwards at the bar of the Assembly. His endowment of a Humanity Chair in St. Leonard's College, St. Andrews, gave great offence to the Regents of St. Salvator's College in the same city, who having no instructor in Roman literature, determined that their more favoured neighbours should not possess their privilege alone.‡ They maintained that the classic learning of St. Leonard's was usurping the domain of philosophy, and so emptying their halls. With a view to the adjusting of differences, and the general reform of the University, the Estates of Parliament, and the General Assembly nominated a joint Commission. Of this body, the Marquis of Argyle, Chancellor of the University, was President, and among the clerical members was the celebrated Alexander Henderson. The complaint of the Regents of St. Salvator and the defence of Sir John Scot occupied the attention of the Commissioners at a meeting held at St. Andrews, on the 10th August, 1642. On this occasion the Commissioners pronounced the following judgment:—

"The Commissioners, considering the Desires and Papers given in

---

* Baillie's Letters and Journals, I. 399.   † Dr. Scott's " Fasti," II., 537.
‡ Report, University Commissioners, 1837, pp. 207 211.

by Sir John Scot of Scots Tarvit, concerning the School of Humanity in St. Leonard's College, and being desirous to cherish every motion that may conduce for advancement of learning and good of the University, but unwilling to settle an inequality in the number of the classes of students betwixt the two Colleges of Philosophie, lest the increase of the one should be a diminution and tend to the ruine of the others, which were a great prejudice to the University in whole:— They do desire the Marquis of Argyle to represent to my Lord Scots-Tarvit their counsel and resolution, beyond which they could not go to this sense, that they think fit that there be a publick Professor of Humanity in St. Leonard's College, to profess publicklie either within that college, or within any other publick place where it should be found expedient, that the Professors of the Old College shall have their leassounes: that this Professor of Humanity shall have for his maintenance an equal portion with the Regents of Philosophie in the new augmentation; that he be called Professor of Humanity; that he teach no scholars in private neither in school nor chamber, because it is intendit the number of the classes in the two colleges be equall, and that by reason of his profession, which is posterior to philosophie, the four Regents of Philosophie have precedencie before him."

Thus the Commissioners attempted a compromise. The new Professor of Humanity was to occupy a rank inferior only to the old Regents of Philosophy, and was equally to share with them in the college revenues. He was to abandon private teaching of every kind, and to impart his prelections in public for the benefit of gownsmen of both colleges. This decision, which was probably acceptable to the Regents of St. Salvator was proportionally obnoxious to those of St. Leonard and induced them to renounce the endowment. Sir John Scot craved the aid of the Commission. His complaint and the decision thereanent are set forth in the following minute:—

"21st March, 1643. The whilk day the Commissioners sitting in full number—the Supplication underwritten was presented whereof the tenor follows: 'To my Lords Commissioners appointed by the late Parlia^t and Generall Assemblie to visit the University, unto your Lo: humbly means and shews Sir John Scot of Scotstarvet, Knight, and one of the Senators of the College of Justice—That whereas out of my love and affection to the advancement of learning I have mortifiet to the College of S^t L's [Leonard's] certain lands rents and books, to the avail of 8000 merks for the use of a Regent of Humanity in the said College, upon special conditions, contaned in a contract betwixt them and me; and in case of failyie of performance of the heads of said contract, the hale sums, lands and books to return to me. And now they finding themselves not able to perform the samen, have subscribed an renunciation, whereof I am yet unwilling to make use of if your Lo's shall be pleased to find out any means how I may have satisfaction; and since inequalitie of the classes in the Philosophie Colleges is pretendit to be the main hindrance, that your Lo's will think upon some way how that may be remedied. Therefore intreat your Lo's to take this to your Lo's consideration and not to suffer so good and charitable a work to perish this way, at the least to be transported to another University, and your Lo's answer.'—Whilk Supplication being read, seen, and considered, and the said Commissioners being therewith well advised, and still desirous to give my Lord Scotstarvet satisfaction in swa far as may not be prejudicial to the University in whole, they have ordained, and be these presents ordain, in addition to their former act, date 10th August, 1642, this offer to be made, that the Master of Humanity in St. Leonard's shall have libertie to take up ane School and teach Scholars in such an indifferent place within the City of St Andrews as the *Senatus Academicus* shall think fit and expedient, providing always that the said Master shall teach no Grammar to his Scholars, and ordained an act to be made hereupon."

The revised ordinance of the Commissioners, though conferring an additional immunity on the Professor of Humanity, rendered nugatory our author's intention in identifying his benefaction with St. Leonard's College. Besides, the Principal and Regents of St. Leonard's, though desirous of retaining the services of a Professor of Humanity, had not obtempered the recommendation of the Commissioners, in allowing the new professor to share in the benefits of the recent grant. Under these circumstances Sir John was justified in recalling his benefaction, and in repossessing himself of his endowment; but still desirous of establishing the chair, he renewed his offer of endowment to the General Assembly. The first portion of the Assembly's Minute on the case is subjoined:—

"Edinburgh, 3d June, 1644. The which day Sir Johne Scot of Scotstarvet, producing the Petition underwritten, together with two Acts of the Commission for Visitation of the Universitie of St. Andrews, the tenour of all which followes: 'Reverend Moderator and remanent Brethren of this General Assembly. Unto your W. shows, I Sir Johne Scot of Scottistarvet, Knight, Director of his Majesties Chancellarie—that when I being moved in the year of God 1620 for the love and favour I did carry to St. Leonard's College in St. Andrews, where I and my umquhile father were educat in Philosophie, to mortifie, for the use of a Regent in Humanitie there, in books land and annual rent, to the avail of 8000 merkis or thereby, which mortification took effect by establishing of umquhile Mr. Alexander Scot and after his decease, of Mr. Robert Norie, present Regent and Professor of Humanitie there, lyke as the said Principall and Regents were in a mutual compact past betwixt them and me, obliged that the said Regent of Humanity should enjoy and be capable of all liberties, privileges and dignities of the Universitie of St. Andrews, and that in an equal degree with themselves: which contract also contained a clause irritant, that if they fail in any point to me, then the mortified lands, books, and annual rent should return back to me as if the same had never been dispensed nor mortified; notwithstanding whereof, at his Majesties last being in this kingdome when he was pleased to bestowe the Priorie of St. Andrews upon the Principals and Regents of the said Universitie, for their better maintenance, the Principal of the said College of St. Leonard's and remanent Com^{rs.} of the Universitie, pretermittit the said Regent of Humanitie in giving up their old Rents, whereby no portion was allotted to him of his Majesty's beneficence, but he altogether by that means secluded therefrom. Lykeas by sentence of the Visitors of the Universitie of St. Andrews, the said Regent was discharged to exercise his function within the said College, and so to have made void that mortification, to the great prejudice of learning, which did move me to raise Summonds of Declarature before the Lords of Councell and Session against them, and thereupon hes obtained sentence, and evicted from them the whole foresaid rent; yet since syne I being informed by the Principal and Regents of the said College of the great ruine and decay which hath followed upon the said College and learning therein through the removing and silencing of the said Regent of Humanity, and being yet unwilling to convert my said donation to any other pious use in any other University nor in the said College of St. Leonard's if the intention of my mortification were duly observed,

Therefore I humbly beseech your W., seriously to considder of the premisses, and of the aforesaid mortification, made in anno 1620, ratified in Parliament anno 1621. Lykeas his Majestie in the act of his first Parliament discharges the inverting of all pious donations, and therefore to give the judgment of the Assembly anent the expedience and necessitie of the said Regent, and his exercise within the said College for the weale thereof, and for the advancement of learning, to be a seminarie of youth to the church and state within this kingdom, declaring what was the intention of the Assembly in anno 1641 in suiting the Commission of Parliament to visit the University; and also to recommend to some of your members to interceid with the ensuing parliament for obtaining their declaration thereanent, and that an Act of Parliament may be obtained for re-establishing the said Regent within the said Colledge in his just integritie, and he to be made participant of his Majestie's munificence with the rest, conform to a particular gift granted be her Majestie under the great seal to him thereanent, whereby others may be encouraged to doe the like in time coming, and your, W's., answer."

With Sir John's wishes the General Assembly complied, and ten days thereafter, viz., on the 13th June, 1644, an Act was passed by the Estates, ratifying the deliverance of the Church, and constituting "a Regent and Professor of Humanity to St. Leonard's College."* This triumph, complete as it was, did not wholly terminate our author's troubles in connexion with St. Leonard's College; for in 1649 Mr. Patrick Robertson, schoolmaster of St. Andrews, complained to the Commission of the General Assembly that he had received "palpable wrong" from the "Regent of Humanity" at St. Leonard's, he having taught "not only all the parts of grammar, but also the very rudiments and elements." The Commission consulted with Sir John, and on his approval ordained that the Regent should abandon his prelections in grammar, under the forfeiture of one hundred marks for each offence, one-half of which sum should be paid to the schoolmaster.† The first occupant of the chair, Mr. Alexander Scot, was probably a relative of the founder. He died prior to June, 1644, when his decease is referred to, and Mr. Robert Norie is named as Professor. In 1747 the colleges of St. Leonard and St. Salvator

---

* Balfour's Annals, iii., 185.
† Report, University Commissioners, 1837, pp. 207—211.

were united by Act of Parliament. Among the Professorships which the Act secured to the United College, that of Humanity was included, the right of nominating to the chair being reserved to the representative of its founder.

In February, 1645, Sir John was appointed one of the Commissioners of Exchequer; but his various and accumulating public duties did not overcome his literary ardour. Interesting himself in the Great Atlas published by Mr. Bleau, he desired that Scotland should be represented in that work. A geographical survey of Scotland was in 1608 commenced by the Rev. Timothy Pont;[*] latterly the undertaking was carried forward under Sir John Scot's pecuniary support.[†] When Mr. Pont died, prior to 1630, his drawings and MSS. fell into the hands of his relatives, who were not careful to preserve them from moths.[‡] At length our author succeeded in procuring them, and he transmitted them to Mr. Bleau with the request that they might be arranged and printed at his expense. On examining the maps Mr. Bleau found that many of them were incomplete, and that descriptions were wanting, indispensable to their forming part of his great work. The drawings being returned to him, Sir John submitted his proposals to Charles I., who readily afforded his royal countenance to an undertaking which was to cost him nothing and might bring credit to his crown. On Sir John's recommendation his Majesty appointed Robert Gordon of Straloch, the ingenious antiquary, to complete the maps and prepare the necessary descriptions. The royal letter to the Laird of Straloch proceeds:—

"To our trustie and weill beloved The Laird of Straloche,

---

[*] Timothy Pont was younger son of the celebrated Mr. Robert Pont, minister of St. Cuthbert's, and one of the Lords of Session. He studied at St. Leonard's College, St. Andrews, and passed M.A. about 1583. He was ordained minister of Dunnet, Orkney, in 1601, and received from his father the lands of Strathmartin, in Forfarshire. In 1609 he obtained a grant of 2,000 acres in the province of Ulster. An expert mathematician and geographer, he entered on his Scottish survey with extraordinary ardour, penetrating on foot into the wildest solitudes. The originals of his maps are preserved in the Advocates Library. His only publication was a Topographical Account of Cunningham, Ayrshire, which was edited for the Maitland Club in 1858.

[†] "Miscellany of the Spalding Club," i., Preface, 37.

[‡] Dr. Scott's "Fasti," iii., 360.

"CHARLES R.

"Trustie and weill beloved We greitt you weill haveing laitly sein certane cairtts of divers schyres of this our ancient kingdome sent heir from Amsterdam to be correctit and helpeitt in the defectis thairof. And being informed of your sufficiencie in that airtt And of your love bothe to Learneing and to the credit of your natioune We have thairfoir thoucht fitt heirby earnestly to intreitt you to taik so mutche paines as to revies the saidis cairtts and to helpe thame in sutche thingis as you find deficient thairintill, that they may be sent back by the directour of our chancellarie to Holland, Quhilk as the samyne will be honorabill for your selff So schall it do us guid and acceptable service. And if occasioun present we schall not be vnmyndfull thairoff. From our palcice of Halyruidhous the aucht day of October 1641."

Straloch undertook the task, and with the assistance of his son, the accomplished James Gordon, Pastor of Rothiemay, David Buchanan * and Sir John Scot himself, brought the work to a completion. In 1645 the first portion of the maps was transmitted to Mr. Bleau, and the autumn of that year found our author on his second visit to the Low Countries.† The following letter addressed by him to the Laird of Straloch expresses his deep concern at the supposed loss of Mr. James Gordon's map of Fifeshire.

"To the Richt honorable, my much respected freind The Laird of Straloch Thais
"Richt honorable
"Being resolved to sie my freinds in the Low Cuntries in this idill tyme for lerning the first rancounter I had at Campheir was that thair I hard that a dunkirker ship had takin your sones cart of fyffe from one of our shipps of Leath callit James Gibson & then instantly I moved one of our cuntry men Mr Trotter to wryt to sum of his friends at ostend quhair the captane then was to persuaid him to send it bak to me heir bot it is feared we sall cum no speid thais pepeill ar so malicius agans our cuntrie. You did wysly that caused your sone keip a doubill of it or vtherways all had been gon. I heir

---

* Nicolson's "Scot. Hist. Library," 18.

† He spent whole days in Bleau's house, at Amsterdam, writing descriptions of the counties from memory. (Bleau's "Atlas," vi., 86.)

by Samuel Wallace that all the carts that are in Jansens hand ar now printed & hourly expects thais that yea heave to finish the work as also he luiks for such descriptiouns as yea can give him & then the buik will go furth without farder. If yea think meet yea may desyre your sone to draw it ouer agane that it may be ioyned with the rest and if yea will give me any buseines heir I sall stryve to obey thame & testifie evir that I am & sall remain

"Your humble servitour

"Campheir 2 *September* 1645.   "Scottistarveit" *

Scotstarvit's visit to the Netherlands was regarded as an affair of state. His voyage to Scotland was undertaken by the government of Zealand, which expressly commissioned a vessel for his use. Such considerate attention to their learned countrymen, the Scottish estates hastened to acknowledge. In his Annals Sir James Balfour records under 6th January, 1646 : †—

"The parl: wreatts a letter to the estaits and Admirall of Zeeland, of thankes for ther kindnes showin to S^r Jo: Scott, in sending a waighter to vafte him ouer to Scotland from the danger of pyratts, wich letter the estaits ordanes in ther name the president of the parliament to subscriue."

In a letter to Straloch Mr. Samuel Wallace of Campvere reports on the "11th of March 1647, ‡ that the cairte § of Fyfe is for the most pairte performit," and that Mr. Bleau has promised "to take no other worck in hand before the illustrations of our kingdome totaliter be performit." Mr. Wallace conveys Mr. Bleau's request, that "he and my Lord Scottistarvit would endeavoire with all possible diligence to assist his porposs be sending vnto hem all quhatsomever kan be gotten, aither for supplie, ornament, decore or illustratione thairof." He writes further :—

"And as for my lord scottistarvit I am sure, that nothing in this world wald be of grytter pleasure and contentment vnto hem but that this worck before his death might be effectuat, having taken so mutch paines in it, and as your honor vrittes vnto me, onles he holdes the matter in hand, I feare it wald be opprest againe, chyflie in these troublesome seasons ; he is now a man kom to grytt aidge, and so is

* Straloch Papers, 52.   † Balfour's "Annals," iii., 351.
‡ Straloch Papers, 54.   § Map.

your honor witch may move us, as it exhortes us to observe our tyme, that ane famous and honorable worck may be broght to light in our dayes; your honor will be pleasit to moue his sone, and all others weel affectuat to this worck, to contribuit ther labors and paines for advancement thairof. I hope the Lord will send vs occasione thairof be a more paceable and setled tyme, seing his maiestie is now kom to holmbye, weel affectuat to agreement with the parliament of Ingland, and they willing thangkfullie to accep thairof and to promote hem to his Royall dignities; the Lord give them grace to remove all dissentiones." In a postscript, Mr. Wallace adds:—" Eftir I vritt this, I receivit a letter from my lord scottistarvet shawes me, that the provost of edenburgh hes send for your sone to drawe the towne of edenburgh, and is to be imployed by the nobilite of Angus to deschryve that shyre; and so I hope he will be advancit be others to grytter worck, if god sendis pace, as be appearance it will be."

Under the title of "Geographiæ Blaevianae Volvmen Sextum," the Scottish Atlas was published at Amsterdam in 1654 in an elegant folio.* The copyright in Britain was secured to Mr. Bleau under the authority of Cromwell.† To Sir John Scot as chief promoter of the undertaking for a period of thirty years, the work was appropriately inscribed, both by the editor and publisher. In an "Address to the Reader," Mr. Bleau writes:—"Opus hoc si nobilissimo ac magnifico viro Ioanni Scoto Scoto-Tarvatio, imputaveris, suam prolem reddes suo patri." Then follows his "Epistle Dedicatory," in which we find these words:—" Ad Ioannem Scotvm, Scoto-Tarvativm vel tibi Scote suum tradebat Scotia nomen, sumebat nomen vel sibi Scote tuum."

Straloch's dedication commences "Amplissimo et magnificentissimo viro Ioanni Scoto;" it is eulogistic throughout. Dated, "9 Cal Februar 1648;" it had, as the following letter from our author will show, been privately submitted for his approval. ‡

---

* Preceding the maps are nineteen discourses relating to the history and general condition of the kingdom, including a long descriptive poem by Andrew Melvill, entitled "Andreae Melvini Scotiæ Topographia."

† According to Nicolson, Bleau dedicated the edition of 1655 to Cromwell, and in the same abused Straloch, omitting several of his best descriptions, particularly those of Aberdeenshire and Banff (Nicolson's "Scot. Hist. Lib.," p. 18).

‡ Straloch Papers, 53.

"To The right honorable my noble freind The laird of Straloch These,

"Right honorable

"I accnaulage that I am not able to render yow thankes for this last fauour that it hath pleased yow to bestoue upon me in wreating that epistle dedicatorie sent hither to me in your last letters yet yow shall not find me wnthankfull if euer it fall in my reach to doe yow or any of yours seruice in thir quarters where I liue. I am with the first occasione to send it to Campher be the meanes of Samuel Wallace to be sent to Amsterdame and referrs it to his discreition to insert it or not insert it at his pleasure, seeing I suspect it will be displeasent to the great men to whom the seuerall mapps ar dedicated, that any epistle of that kynd should be prefixed to such a worke, bearing the nam of such a mean man as I am.*

"The Earle of Southeask hath intention to send for Mr James [Gordon] in the spring to draue the shyre of Angus and aught in reason so to doe seeing he lost Mr Timothies mapp† and I hope ye will be a councellor of him to come that the work may be the soner perfected and brought to a wished end, and not be left defectiue in the want of so good a shyre. As concerning that, that ye can not find the genologie of houses, aduertish me what ye want and I shall endeuore to furnish yow for I haue besyd me a not of all charters from King Robert Bruice dayes to this present, wherby I may give yow satisfaction in that poynt I pray yow send me what descriptiones ye haue ready till then and alwayes I shall continowe

"Your humble servitour

"Edinburgh 2 *February* 1648.　　　　　　　"Scottistarveit."

In his description of Fifeshire, Straloch is thus particular in recording Sir John's munificence to St. Leonard's College :—

"In hoc ornando singularis enituit munificentia nobilissimi ingeniorum fautoris D Iohannis Scoti, Scoto-Tarvatii, Equitis aurati, quum prioribus professionibus philosophicis novam super-addiderit humaniorum literarum seu eloquentiæ, stipendio liberali

---

* Nearly all the maps in Bleau's Atlas are inscribed to leading noblemen, whose armorial escutcheons are elegantly emblazoned on them.

† The Earl of Southesk had not fulfilled his intention, for the map of Angus (Forfarshire) does not appear in Bleau's Atlas.

collato, quod perpetuum esse voluit : cujus etiam liberalitate ingens incrementum experta est Collegii publica Bibliotheca."

In completing the Scottish Atlas, Straloch received the protection of the civil and military authorities—being exempted by them from public imposts. The following documents refer to this immunity.*

"Exemption gevin be the parleament 28 *Januar* 1646

"My lords of parliament unto your lordships humblie means and shows I your lordships servitor Mr. Robert Gordoune of Straloche that quhair in consideratione of my pains and travill in reviseinge and correcting thee cartts of this kingdome it pleasit your lordships to exeem mee from the ordinare burdens of the rest of thee subjectis in Scotland to thee end I might thee better attend thairupone and bee encouraged therby to len my best asistance for the perfectione of soe honorable a worke whilke albeit I have cairfullie gone about hitherto and ame radie to give a prove thairof to thos who hes the doinge of the worke of this kingdome yitt my former warrand is misregarded by the present commanders and I daylie taxed in a heavie manner wherby I will be discouraged and dissinabled frome prosecuteing thee intendit worke except your lordships provyde remead Hearfor I beseache your lordships to take consideratione of the premisses and to cause renew my saids warrand and exemptione in suche a mainer that it may bee valable for mee to free mee frome other warrands of comanders who hes slighted your former commands whiche will encourage mee more and more to folowe out thee intendit worke and to be radie at all occasions to obey your lordships commandiment and your lordships answeare humblie I crave."

"St Andrews 28 *January* 1646

"The Comitte of despatches haveing considered the supplication abovewrittin do vpon the grounds therin mentioned renew all former acts and warrants past in the supplicants favors And ordaines all officers and sogers punctually to observe the samyn as they will be answerable vpon thair heyest perells

"JA PRYMEROSE."

"At Aberdein the second day of *March* 1646.

"The quhilk day the seueral actis and warrands respectiue aboue-

* Straloch Papers, 56–7.

writtin were producit befoir the Committee of warr for the shyre of Aberdein and being sein and considered be theme, they acknowledge the same and does recommend the foirsaides warrands to Colonell Robert Montgomerie comander in chefe

"Mr Tho: Merser"

In obtaining ecclesiastical support Straloch and his patron were less fortunate. Sir John presented "a supplication" to the General Assembly, entreating that certain ministers in each province might be appointed to furnish descriptions of their several districts, and the application was approved and appointments made. But few of the clergy responded, and the materials obtained from those who did were very inconsiderable. In applying for statistics to the parochial clergy, Sir John Scot, it may be remarked, became pioneer of a national work, the "Statistical Account of Scotland," which a century and a half afterwards was carried out under the auspices of Sir John Sinclair.

Having discharged the heavy costs of engraving the Scottish maps, Sir John devised another outlet for his munificence. Claiming descent from the West of Scotland * he resolved to bestow a benefaction on the city of Glasgow as the western capital. In that city a fire † had deprived a thousand families of their homes, and a collection on behalf of the sufferers had been made throughout the kingdom. This event ‡ confirmed Sir John's intention of making a permanent endowment in the city. He conveyed to the magistrates and council the lands of Peckie, § in the parish of St. Leonard's and

---

* Sir John's connexion with the West of Scotland was, it is believed, through his maternal grandmother.

† The fire took place on the 17th June, 1652. About eighty alleys were destroyed, and the corporation apprehended that, without foreign help, the city would be ruined.—Dr. Strang's Bursaries, &c., of Glasgow, 71—74.

‡ In his bequest, addressed to the magistrates and town council of Glasgow, dated 7th and 13th June, 1653, and in a second contract, dated 28th April, 1658, Sir John refers to "the love he had for the city, being the finest city of the west, out of which country he descended, and in consideration of the calamity of the inhabitants through fire."—Dr. Strang's Bursaries.

§ The farm of Peckie, or Peckie Mill, is situated about four miles south-east of St. Andrews, and lies between the estate of Kenly Green and the lands of Kenly, the latter belonging to St. Salvator's College, St. Andrews. It consists of about 104 acres, chiefly arable.

county of Fife, for the purpose of " putting poor boys to apprenticeships to any lawful honest trade or calling," the magistrates binding themselves to admit them as burgesses, free of charge. At first, four boys were maintained as apprentices, three being presented by the donor and his successors, and one by the corporation. By Act of Council, 5th April, 1781, an agreement was made between David Scott, of Scotstarvet, by which it was provided, that when the lands should yield a yearly rent of Thirty Pounds, Mr. Scott should have the right to present four boys, and the Council two.

Owing to altered circumstances, the teaching of apprentices by paying fees to masters became unnecessary, and in 1797 the corporation and Sir John's representatives agreed, that in lieu of apprentice fees, twelve boys should be placed for education in one of the local seminaries. The proceeds of the lands of Peckie, amounting at present to £126 a year, are paid annually by the town council of Glasgow to the managers of Wilson's school for the education of twelve youths, who are styled Scotstarvet's boys.*

In 1648 and 1649 Sir John served on the Committee of War. Though keenly opposed to the ecclesiastical policy of Charles I., he was attached to the monarchy. Considerably after the commencement of the Civil War, his brother-in-law, William Drummond of Hawthornden, composed at Scotstarvet† his History of Scotland and his numerous tracts in favour of royalty. In an address to the noblemen, barons, and gentlemen of Scotland, written in 1639, Drummond predicted that during the impending troubles there might probably arise one who " would name himself PROTECTOR of the liberty of the kingdom, but who would surcharge greater miseries than those of the past, and who, though calling himself Protector of the Church, should be without learning, and under the pretence of zeal and piety, commit a thousand iniquities and bring all into confusion." A prediction of this sort was not likely to escape the vigilant eye of Cromwell, who, seeing that its author had passed away,‡ was the more likely to associate with its utterance the individual from whose

---

* We are indebted to the City Chamberlain of Glasgow for an account of the present condition of the charity.

† Sage's "Life of Drummond."

‡ William Drummond of Hawthornden, died 4th December, 1649. He experienced a severe shock on the execution of Charles I., from which he did not recover.

residence it had emanated. Sir John was deprived of his offices, and fined £1500 sterling.

Under his wrongs, Sir John complained frequently. At length a prospect of redress was opened up by his securing the influence of General Monk. The following letter from the General to Secretary Thurloe, dated " Dalkeith, 1st October, 1658," will explain the position of affairs at that period.*

" My Lord,—S^r· John Scott of Scottis-Tarvutt, having guift from the late king under the great seale, for the place of director of the chancery in Scotland for life, and the said place being disposed of by the Comissioners from the Parliament in the year 1651, hee made fower severall addresses to his late highness, at the last wherof it was found by the Comissioners of the great seale, Sir Thomas Widdrington, the lord Montague the lord Whitlock and Col. Sydenham, to whom his Highness referred the cognition thereof, that they found no cause why hee should have bin displaced out of that office, the same being only ministeriall. But upon his last petition, seeking to be restored, his highnes would give no determined answer till hee had advised with his councill, the cause whereof was because he had given a guift of the same before to one Alexander Jaffray (not having understood of Sir John Scott his right thereto) and now Mr Jaffray being very siche, Sr John and myself make itt our request unto you that your lordshippe will be pleased to stand his friend to his highnesse, that in case Mr Jaffray should dye, his highnesse will not dispose of the said place of director of the Chancery, till he hath heard S^r· John Scott speake for himselfe. I crave your Lordshipp's pardon for guieving you this trouble, and remain
Your Lordshippes most humble servant
GEORGE MONCK."

The answer to General Monk's letter has not been preserved. Alexander Jaffray had on the recommendation of Cromwell's judges been constituted Director of the Chancery in March, 1652, with a salary of £200 sterling. At the same time he received £1,500 sterling (precisely the amount of the penalty inflicted on his predecessor) as a portion of the debt incurred by him in waiting as one of the Scottish commissioners on Charles II. in Holland in 1650. He

---

* Thurloe's " State Papers," vii., 421.

had been Chief Magistrate of Aberdeen, and representative of that city in the Scottish Parliament. He subsequently became a member of Cromwell's Parliament. He died on the 5th May, 1673. Some years before his death he became a zealous member of the Society of Friends.*

While Sir John was a severe sufferer under the Commonwealth, it is interesting to remark that the Poems of his brother-in-law, the upholder of kings, were during that period first printed in a collected form by Edward Phillips, nephew of the poet Milton, the Protector's Latin Secretary.† The volume is accompanied by a Latin dedication to our author, whose merits are set forth both in prose and verse.

The Restoration, propitious to so many friends of General Monk, was the precursor of fresh troubles to the Laird of Scotstarvet. The directorship of the Chancery was bestowed on Sir William Ker, who, as Sir John remarked, "danced him out of office, being a dextrous dancer." He was besides mulct‡ in a considerable penalty as a supposed supporter of the old regime. In the Act containing exceptions from the Act of Indemnity, passed in 1662, he is fined "six thousand pundis," or £500 sterling.§ Disheartened by this cruel treatment, which he ascribed to "the power and malice of his enemies,"‖ he returned to Scotstarvet,¶ there, in the congenial intercourse of learned friends, to close his eventful life.

According to Nisbet, men of learning came to him from all quarters, "so that his house became a kind of college."** At Scotstarvet he composed his "Staggering State," a work which was not published by himself or any of his representatives, and which it is likely he did not intend for indiscriminate perusal. He died at Scotstarvet in 1670 at the age of eighty-four.†† His remains were, it is supposed, interred in the parish church of Kinghorn, where he possessed a right of sepulture.‡‡ His will was, on the 11th

---

* Diary and Memoir of Alexander Jaffray, by John Barclay, London, 1733, 8vo., *passim*.

† The volume is entitled, "The Poems of that most famous wit, Mr. William Drummond, of Hawthornden," 1656. 8vo.

‡ Brunton and Haig, 281.   § Act Parl. vii., 421.

‖ "Staggering State."   ¶ Situated in the parish of Ceres, Fifeshire.

** Nisbet's "Heraldry," ii., 293.   †† Douglas's Baronage, 222.

‡‡ On the 17th May, 1642, the Kirksession of Kinghorn assigned "to Sir Jhone Scott of Scotstarvet, and his wyfe and children for sepulture in the south-east

February, 1671, confirmed at Edinburgh to Walter Scott of Lethan, his third son, the eldest then living. Sir John had disposed of his heritable property during his life, and he made no bequests. In "an eik" or codicil is mentioned a bond to William Dick, merchant, Edinburgh, bearing date 28th April, 1621, which contained an assignation granted by Mr. Dick, in favour of Sir J. Scot for £1000 Scots, and which with interest amounted to £4695 Scots. The cautioners to this bond were Capt. William Scott, Walter, Earl of Buccleuch, Lord Scott of Whitchester, and John Scott of Sintoun.*

Sir John was three times married. His first wife was Anne, daughter of Sir John Drummond of Hawthornden, by his wife, Anne, daughter of Robert Lord Elphinstone; she bore him two sons and seven daughters. Secondly, he married Margaret, daughter of Sir James Melvill of Hallhill, by whom he had one son. His third wife was Margaret, daughter of H. Monypenny of Pitmilly, and relict of Rigg of Artherny; she bore him one son. Sir John's eldest son, James, became conjunct Director of Chancery, and was knighted by Charles I. He predeceased his father in 1650, and was succeeded by his elder son, James, born August 1644, and who, dying without issue in 1668, was succeeded by his only brother David. On the 3rd November 1668, David Scott,† was served heir male to his brother in "the lands of Tarvitt," and "the lands of Caiplie, Thirdpart, and Wester Pitcorthie, "in the parish of Kilrenny, "all united in the barony of Scotstarvitt."

Prudent and conversant with rural affairs, David Scott largely improved the family estates. He married first, Nicolas, eldest daughter of Sir John Grierson of Lag, by whom he had one daughter Marjery, who became wife of David, fifth Lord Stormount. He

---

part of the church, extending in lenght sexten foot from the east end westward, and fyftin foot of breadth from the south wall to the partition wall of the quier." Sir John was proprietor of Pitmeadie, in Kinghorn parish, and had claimed a right of interment in the church (Kirk Session Records of Kinghorn).

* William Dick, a wealthy Edinburgh merchant, and Lord Provost of the city, was in January, 1642, created a baronet of Nova Scotia. He gave large loans to Charles I., and afterwards to escape annoyance gave £64,934 sterling to the Parliament. He was thrown into prison by Cromwell, and died at Westminster, 19th December, 1655, in a condition of poverty.

† "Inquisitiones Speciales," Fife, 1046.

married, secondly, Elizabeth, daughter of John Ellies of Ellieston, by whom he had a son, David, his heir, and two daughters, Marjery and Elizabeth. Marjery Scot married Peter Ogilvy of Balfour, and her sister Elizabeth became wife of Alexander, Earl of Balcarres. David Scott of Scotstarvet died in 1718 in his 73rd year.*

John Scot, second son of our author, received from his father a grant of half the lands of Gibleston, in the parish of Carnbee, in which, on his death in 1657, he was succeeded by his son George.†

Additional births in our author's family are in his family Bible,‡ recorded thus:—

"George Scott, sone to Sr. Johne Scott, of Scottstarvitt, who borne in Pittodie the 19th of Aprill, 1643.

"Walter Scott, sone to Sir John Scott, of Scottistervett, was borne in Edinburgh the 7 of January, 1649.

"Le Sr. Jacques Scot de Tarvet a et son fils nomine Jacques que fut batizè en Angus le 1 Sep. 1664."

David Scott, of Scotstarvet, who died in 1718, was succeeded by his son David, an advocate at the Scottish Bar, and M.P. for Fifeshire. He married Lucy, daughter of Sir Robert Gordon, of Gordonston, baronet, by whom he had two sons and two daughters. Elizabeth, the elder daughter, married Peter Hay, of Leys; Lucy, the younger, died unmarried.

David Scott, the elder son, succeeded his father, and John, the younger, joined the army, in which he attained the rank of Major-

---

* Douglas's Baronage, 224. † "Inquisitiones Speciales," Fife, 867.

‡ A Bible which belonged to Sir John Scot, and in which the births of certain members of the family are recorded, has, though in the hands of strangers, been carefully preserved. It is a thick folio, with the text in French and Latin, bearing the title, "Latino-gallica la Bible Francoise-latine, 1568." At the back of the title-page is attached a printed book-slip with these words:—"Mr. Iohn Scot, Director our Soueraigne Lords Chancellarie," and on the last blank page of the volume are the entries quoted above with those following:—

"Sir James Scott, of Tarvett, had a sone baptised, named James, in Angus, in the parish of Enderkillour, the beginning of Sept. 1644.

"William Scott, sone to Mr. George Scott, of Pittodie, was borne the 7 day of Feb. 1666 years."

Sir John's Bible was purchased by Principal Lee at the book sale of Professor Flint, of St. Andrews. At the Principal's own sale it was purchased by Mr. Adam Sim, of Coulter Mains, at whose sale in 1869 it was knocked down for 2s. 6d. to Mr. Levy, Prince's Street, Edinburgh.

General. Having retired from military service he established his residence at Balcomie, parish of Crail, Fifeshire. About 1768 he was elected M.P. for Fife. He espoused first, Lady Mary Hay, eldest daughter of James, thirteenth Earl of Erroll, which marriage was dissolved. He married secondly, Margaret, youngest daughter of Robert Dundas, of Arniston, Lord President of the Court of Session, by Henrietta Baillie, heiress of Lamington; she died in 1795. Major-General Scott died suddenly at Balcomie in December 1775. His remains were interred in the churchyard of Kilrenny, where a magnificent monument, erected by his daughter, the Duchess of Portland, denotes his grave. The monument is uninscribed. General Scott was a noted gambler, and consequent on his success at play, became owner of numerous estates. At the period of his death he was regarded as the wealthiest commoner in Scotland. Her succession is said to have availed his eldest daughter £25,000 a year.

By his second marriage General Scott left three daughters, Henrietta, Lucy, and Joan. By the death of her uncle, David Scott, of Scotstarvet, Henrietta, the eldest, became heir of line to Sir John Scot, of Scotstarvet, and representative of the family. She married, 4th August, 1795, William Henry Cavendish, Marquess of Titchfield, who succeeded his father as fourth Duke of Portland, 30th October, 1809. Henrietta Scott, Duchess of Portland, had four sons, William Henry, Marquess of Titchfield, who died 4th March, 1821, aged twenty-eight; William John Cavendish Scott Bentinck, now Duke of Portland; Lord George Frederick, the distinguished politician, who died unmarried 21st September, 1848; and Lord Henry William. Of the Duchess's four daughters, Charlotte, third daughter, was, 14th July, 1827, married to the Right Honourable John Evelyn Denison, of Ossington, Notts, afterwards Speaker of the House of Commons. The Duchess died 28th April, 1844.

Lucy, second daughter of Major-General Scott, married, 26th February, 1795, Francis Stuart, Lord Doune, who 28th August, 1810, succeeded his father as ninth Earl of Moray; she died 3rd August, 1798, leaving two sons, Francis and John, who were successively tenth and eleventh Earls of Moray. Both died unmarried.

Joan, youngest daughter of General Scott, married, 8th July, 1800, George Canning, the distinguished statesman, on whose death,

8th August, 1827, she was created Viscountess Canning. Her ladyship died 15th March, 1837, and was succeeded in the peerage by her only surviving son, Charles John, Viscount Canning, who as Governor-General of India during the Mutiny acquired distinction; he was raised to the Earldom of Canning 21st May, 1859. Earl Canning died *s. p.* 17th July, 1862, when the family honours became extinct.

A SHORT ACCOUNT OF THE OFFICERS OF STATE, AND OTHER GREAT OFFICERS IN SCOTLAND.

BY WALTER GOODAL.

In all the nations whose governments were framed upon the model of the feudal institutions, or by whom the feudal laws were adopted, as the spirit of these laws contributed much to the aggrandizing the prince, and impressing an awe and veneration of the government; so no other means were thought to be more effectual for this purpose than the conferring of splendour and dignity upon the prime officers employed by the prince in the execution of his government, which reflected back again with double lustre upon the throne, as the fountain from which these honours and dignities originally flowed. And most of these nations had a very great conformity and resemblance with one another in the names and institutions of these great officers, or Officers of the Crown, as they were called, which were generally seven in number, and ranked in the following order. 1. The High Constable. 2. The High Admiral. 3. The High or Great Chancellor. 4. The Great Justiciar. 5. The Great Chamberlain. 6. The Great Protonotary. 7. The Great Seneschal or Steward.

These several offices appeared first in the greatest splendour in France, after the suppression of the office of *Maire de palais*, into which the execution of almost the whole business of the administration was engrossed. They were afterwards adopted into the government of the Two Sicilies; and the great offices of Scotland, in our ancient constitution, bore a very great resemblance to those of these nations, both as to their names and powers.

In the time of King Malcolm II. it is presumable there were no more of these great offices extant, but those of the Chancellor, the Justice-General, the Chamberlain, the Steward, the Constable and the Marischal; for, in his laws, the fees of these are particularly appointed, and they are ranked in the above order; and no more are mentioned.

At that time, and long after, these were called Officers of the Crown, as some think, to distinguish them from the other great officers which were called OF THE STATE. However that be, the distinction came at length to be lost, and they were all known indiscriminately as Officers of the State or Officers of the Crown; and certain privileges came to be annexed to them, particularly, that in all acts or meetings concerning the State they sat as members, by virtue of their office, as in Parliaments, Conventions, &c., and got the title of Lords prefixed to the name of their office. And, in the Act xxxi. Parl. ii. James VI., the following are enumerated as Officers of the Crown, viz., the Treasurer, Secretary, Collector, Justice-General, Justice-Clerk, Advocate, Master of Requests, Clerk of Register, Director of the Chancery, and Directory of the Rolls.

Afterwards, in the year 1617, King James, in privy council, declared that in that, and all other parliaments, eight only should sit as Officers of State, and these he ranked as follows: Treasurer, Privy Seal, Secretary, Clerk-Register, King's Advocate, Justice-Clerk, Treasurer-Depute, Master of Requests.

The other great officers, which were omitted among the Officers of State, might still very properly be called Officers of the Crown, as the Chancellor, Constable, Admiral, Chamberlain and Great Justiciar, as these offices still remained, and with pretty extensive powers.

To give a short account of the nature of these several offices, and the others mentioned in the following history, is the design of this introduction; and we shall begin in the order mentioned in King Malcolm's laws.

I.—OF THE CHANCELLOR.

The first office there mentioned is that of Chancellor, which was the second in dignity in France, and was much the same as the *Quæstor* among the Romans. He was chief in matters of justice, as the Constable was in those of war; *legum Conditor, regalis consilii Particeps, justitiæ Arbiter.*

In England, the Chancellor is principal judge in the high-court of equity, and presides in the House of Peers; his office is conferred upon him by delivery of the great seal, of which he is keeper *ratione officii.*

In the laws of King Malcolm II. the Chancellor is placed before all the other officers; and from these it appears that he had the principal direction of the Chancery, or Chancellary as it was called, which was his proper office. His constant province was the custody of the king's seal, and he was the king's most intimate counsellor, as appears from an old law cited by Sir James Balfour in his Practicks, p. 15. " The Chancellar sall at all tymes assist the king, in giving him counsall mair secretly nor the rest of the nobilitie, to quhais ordinances all officiaris, als well of the realme as of the kingis hous, sould answer and obey. The Chancellar sall be ludgit neir unto the kingis grace, for keiping of his bodie, and the seill; and that he may be readie baith day and nicht at the kingis command." By having the custody of the great seal, he had an opportunity of examining the king's grants and other deeds, which were to pass under it, and to cancel them if they appeared to be against law, and obtained by subreption or false suggestions; and from this seems to be derived the name *Cancellarius*. There are some instances wherein it appears the Chancellor had not the keeping of the great seal; but these are very rare.

King James VI. ordained the Chancellor to have the first place and rank in the nation, *ratione officii;* by virtue whereof he presided in the parliament and in all courts of judicature. After the restoration of King Charles II. by a particular declaratory law, Parl. I., the Lord Chancellor was declared, by virtue and right of his office, president in all the meetings of parliament, or other public judicatures of the kingdom. Though this act was made with an intention to declare the Chancellor president of the Exchequer, as well as other courts, yet, in 1663, the king declared the Treasurer to be president of that court, and not the Chancellor.

II.—Of the Director of Chancery.

The Chancery, from the above-mentioned laws of King Malcolm II., appears to have been no other than the proper office of the Chancellor, the writs there mentioned being such as to this day have a relation to that office: but it appears to have been early taken from under his inspection and put under the inspection of another officer, by the name of the Director of the Chancery. Originally all summonses were issued from this office but now the business there is confined to issuing the precepts, brieves, such as of mortancestry, furiosity, &c., and the writing out of those writs in a peculiar fixed form, to which the king's great seal is to be appended. The Director of Chancery also adjusts the responde-book, by which the sheriffs account to the Exchequer, for the non-entry, and other duties exigible by them from the heirs of vassals, at their entry to their estates. The keeping of the quarter-seal, or testimony of the great seal, as it is called, is also committed to him; by this seal, precepts of sasine upon charters under the great seal were sealed, and certain other writs.

III.—Of the Great Justiciar, or Justice-General.

This office, in foreign states, was originally next to the High Chancellor, who was called the Magistrate of Magistrates, and Head of all the Officers of Justice; but in process of time, particular justices being appointed for the several provinces, subordinate to the Great Justiciar, and their proceedings subject to his review, he came to be considered as next to the Constable in rank and dignity, and all causes, civil as well as criminal, became competent to him, high treason not excepted.

In Scotland the Great Justiciar, or Justice-General, was placed next the Chancellor, *L. Reg. Malc.*, and his court was originally the only sovereign court of the nation, and had a great part of that jurisdiction which the Session hath now: and, even after the erection of the Court of Session, several civil causes came before it, *Reg. Maj. l.* 1, *c.* 5, and *l.* 2, *c.* 74. But at length his jurisdiction came to be restricted to criminal causes only, by several statutes, by which he had power to name his own deputes.

In the year 1671 the Court of Justiciary was constituted, as it now stands, by a commission under the great seal, afterwards ratified by the regulations 1672, whereby it is made to consist of the Justice-General, who is constant president, the Justice-Clerk, and five of the ordinary Lords of Session, and they declared to be the supreme ordinary judges in criminals.

After King Malcolm's times, Scotland was divided into two justiciaries, one upon the south side of Forth, who was called *Justitiarius Lothianiæ*, and in old charters *Judex Laudoniæ*, and the other on the north side of Forth.

This office was anciently possessed heritably by several families, and last of all by the family of Argyle, who surrendered it *in anno* 1628 by contract, which was ratified in parliament *in anno* 1633. It was afterwards constituted by a gift under the great seal, either *ad vitam*, or by a temporary commission. By King Malcolm's laws the salary was of old five pounds for every day of the Justice-ayr.

IV.—OF THE JUSTICE-CLERK.

By the forementioned laws of King Malcolm II. it appears that the Justice-Clerk was then no other than clerk to the Justiciar: but, by the foresaid act of King James VI., by which he is declared one of the officiars of the crown, it seems he was then esteemed an officer of importance. Sir George Mackenzie is of opinion he was at that time one of the ordinary judges of the court. Others allege that he was not a judge before the year 1663, when he was declared to be so by an act of the Privy Council. However, by the regulations 1672, above-mentioned, he is now a constituent member of that bench, and always presides in absence of the Justice-General; and to this day he names the Clerk of Justiciary and his Depute.

V.—OF THE GREAT CHAMBERLAIN.

This was the fifth great officer in the feudal governments, and the same with the High Treasurer, or superintendent of the finances, in later ages; it is reckoned the same with the *Præpositus Sacri Cubiculi*, mentioned by Justinian, and equalled by him to the *Præfectus Prætorio*, and placed *inter illustres Palatinos*. In France he was called *Grand Chambrier*, and it was constantly possessed by the family of Bourbon.

He is ranked by King Malcolm as the third great officer, and called *Camerarius Domini Regis;* and had a salary of £200 allotted him. He anciently collected the revenues of the crown, at least before we had a Treasurer, of which office there is not any vestige till the restoration of King James I., and he disbursed the money necessary for the maintenance of the king's household.

He had a jurisdiction for judging of all crimes committed within burgh, and of the crime of forestalling; and was in effect Justice-General over the burrows, and was to hold Chamberlain-ayrs every year for that effect, the form whereof is set down in a tract called *Iter Camerarii*, the Chamberlain-ayr, among our old laws in *Reg. Majest*. He was a supreme judge, nor could his decrees be questioned by any inferior judicatory. His sentences were to be put in execution by the bailies of burghs. He also settled the prices of provisions within burgh, and the fees of the workmen in the mint-house.

Home, in his history of the Douglasses, says, that the Chamberlain-ayr became very odious to the burrows, being rather a legal robbery than a court of justice. And the lords who seized King James VI. at Ruthven, 24th August, 1582, commonly called The Raid of Ruthven, issued a proclamation in the King's name, discharging the Chamberlain-ayrs to be kept; but this was chiefly *in odium* of the Duke of Lennox, then heritable Chamberlain, who was of the opposite faction, and was then banished.

The privileges of this office had fallen much into desuetude, not having been exercised for many years by the family of Lennox; and at last, in 1703, the duke resigned it in Queen Anne's hands, *ad perpetuam remanentiam*, since which time no Chamberlain has been appointed.

VI.—OF THE HIGH STEWARD.

The next great office was the High Steward. In the foreign states he is ranked the last of the great officers. He was judge of the King's household, and the whole family of the royal palace was under his care.

In Scotland his province was of the same nature: for in King Malcolm's laws, in which he is ranked in the fourth place, the other officers of the King's household, as the butler, baker, &c., are subjoined to him, and have their fees specified; and those of all the other inferior officers are left to the Steward's discretion.

It was reckoned an office of very great dignity, and was held heritably for many years by one family, who at last got the name of the officer settled as a sirname upon their posterity by Walter, the son of Alan, who was at the same time Justiciar to King Alexander II. *anno* 1230. They were frequently nearly allied to the crown, and at last succeeded to it in the person of Robert, eldest son to Walter Steward, in the year 1371. This Robert was ninth heritable Lord High Steward of Scotland, and his son John, afterwards King Robert III., was created, by his father, Prince and Steward of Scotland, since which time the eldest son of the king is *natus Senescallus Scotiæ*.

VII.—OF THE HIGH CONSTABLE.

The High Constable, in France and other foreign nations, held the first place among the great officers. He was called *Comes stabuli, et regalium præpositus equorum.* His two chief prerogatives were, first, the keeping of the king's sword, which the king at his promotion, when he swears fealty, delivers to him, in imitation of Trajan, who delivered his naked sword to Suro Licinius, his *Præfectus prætorio,* with these words, *Accipe hunc ensem, ut si quidem recte reip. imperavero, pro me; sin autem secus, in me utaris:* from which these words, with a little variation, *pro me, si mereor in me,* were, with a naked sword put by Buchanan on the money coined during the minority of King James VI. Hence the badge of the Constable is a naked sword, as it was likewise of the *Præfectus prætorio* in the Roman empire. His other prerogative was the absolute and unlimited command of the king's armies while in the field; but that did not extend to castles and garrisons.

The High Constable with us was, by the laws of King Malcolm II., *c.* 6, judge to all crimes committed within two leagues of the king's house, or four Scots miles. Skeen, in his treatise of crimes, says, "All transgressions committed within the wand of the king's Marschal, *i.e.,* within twa leagues to the king's person (which is called the chalmer of peace) pertains to the constable, *leg.* Malcolm II., *c.* 6, in which place this jurisdiction is attributed to the Marischal, and constable; and in some old books it is noted to pertain to the marischal in time of warfare, and to the constable in time of peace."

The jurisdiction of this office came at last to be exercised only as to crimes during the time of parliament, which some extended likewise to all general conventions.

It has stood heritably in the family of Errol, since the time of King Robert Bruce, *vid.* Sir G. Mackenzie's criminals, *part* 2., *tit.* 4.

VIII.—OF THE MARISCHAL.

The Marischal is reckoned to be originally a German word and office, *a maker of camps,* and the ax, which he bears as the badge of his office, was that instrument with which he broke the ground; though this part of his office came to be delegated to the *Marischal du camp.* The Marischal commanded the cavalry, whereas the Constable commanded the whole army; yet, as Tillet observes, the Marischal was not under the Constable, else he could not be an officer of the crown; for it is essential to all officers of the crown and of the state to depend upon none but the king. Of old the orders in military cases were directed *To our Constable and Marischal,* and in

King Malcolm's laws his jurisdiction is conjoined with that of the Constable.

The office of Marischal has never been out of the family of Keith, and they have had no other title than that of Earls Marishal.

IX.—OF THE HIGH ADMIRAL.

This officer bore the second rank next after the Constable in the Italian states, first, because in the feudal governments the warlike officers were of greater use, and more esteemed than those of peace; and then, as a great part of their wars were carried on against the Saracens by sea, the office of Admiral, or chief commander by sea, came to be considered as of nearly equal importance with that of the Constable, or General by land. His command was very extensive, comprehending not only the king's ships and sailors, but he had also the inspection of the ports, harbours, and sea-coasts, and he had a particular tribunal, where the judges appointed by him decided all causes relating to sea affairs, and that according to a particular body of naval law.

In Scotland the ancient powers of the High Admiral are pretty much the same. He is properly the king's lieutenant and justice-general upon the seas, and his jurisdiction as a judge extended to the trial of all crimes committed at sea, and to all controversies, actions and quarrels concerning crimes, faults and trespasses committed upon sea, or in the ports and creeks thereof, or in fresh waters and navigable rivers, so far as the sea flows and ebbs; this he exercises by a depute, commissioned by him, called the Depute-judge-admiral, who likewise judges in matters purely commercial as arising from the sea.

Hepburn, Earl of Bothwell, was made heritable Admiral in Scotland, and upon his forfeiture, Stewart, Earl of Bothwell, had the office conferred upon him, and he also being forfeited, in 1603, King James gave it to the Duke of Lennox. But his male line having failed, King Charles II., on whom the succession devolved as heir of line, conferred it on his natural son, whom he created Duke of Lennox and Richmond, who, in the year 1703, resigned that office as well as that of heritable Chamberlain of Scotland in the hands of Queen Anne, *ad perpetuam remanentiam.*

X.—OF THE SECRETARY.

This office in Scotland was nearly the same with that of the great Protonotary, which agreed with the *Primicerius notariorum* among the Romans; these were of the prince's council, and acted therein as his secretaries. He was constantly to attend the king's person, receive the petitions and memorials that were presented to him, and write the king's answers upon them. All letters patent passed through his hands, and were drawn up by him. And with us all the king's letters and dispatches, warrants, orders, &c., were wrote out by him, and generally subscribed by him; and where the writings were long a short docquet was also subscribed by him for the king's perusal, to show what the writings were, and the king afterwards superscribed them; and all the writings signed by the king came through his hands, he was answerable for them if they contained any thing derogatory to the laws or the dignity of the crown. He was called *Clericus Regis*, though some apply that to the Clerk-Register.

XI.—OF THE MASTER OF REQUESTS.

We have no Master of Requests now, that charge being swallowed up by the secretary's office. Their business with us was, as at Rome, to represent to the king the complaints of the people; *Referendarii*, says Cassiodore, *lib. 6. dolores alienos asserunt, conquerentium vota satiant, and per eos judices corriguntur.*

XII.—OF THE TREASURER.

This office was first known in Scotland upon King James I., his return from England, when he made a High Treasurer as well as a Chamberlain, who was now confined solely to the government of the burrows; and the management of the king's revenue was committed to the care of the Treasurer as a distinct officer of state. His business was to examine and pass the accompts of the sheriffs, and others concerned in levying the revenues of the crown: he also received resignations of lands, and other subjects in use to be resigned in the king's hands, and to revise, compound, and pass signatures, gifts of tutory, &c. All which is now committed to the Court of exchequer in Scotland.

In 1617 the Treasurer is ranked by King James VI. as first officer of state; and in 1623, when he determined the precedency of his counsellors, he is ranked next to the Chancellor, and in 1663 was declared president of the Exchequer.

The office of Comptroller, which was sometimes joined with that of Treasurer, and designed *computorum rotulator*, and that of collector of the new augmentations, which were both distinct offices from that of the Treasurer, were all conjoined into one by King James, and exercised by the Treasurer till 1685, when the treasury was put in commission.

The Treasurer-depute was considered in the Treasurer's absence as Treasurer himself, and claimed precedency accordingly.

XIII.—OF THE KING'S SEAL, PARTICULARLY THE PRIVY SEAL.

Of old, in the attesting of writs, seals were commonly adhibited in place of the subscription, and this took place even in documents of debt as well as in writs of the more solemn kind, as charters, which appears from the books of *The Majesty*, L. 3, C. 8. But from the same place it appears that inconveniences began very early to arise from that practice, and writing becoming more frequent, it is now gone much into desuetude, at least, is only used as one of the many solemnities introduced by the law for certiorating deeds.

In writs granted by the king the affixing of his seal alone gave them sufficient authority without signing. This seal was generally kept by the Chancellor: and from the old law cited above, p. 15, it may be inferred that all the king's despatches were verified by it.

In later times, when business increased, and particularly after King James I. returned from his captivity in England, and set about the modelling his court after the forms he had seen followed in the court of England, he appointed several new officers, and assigned them distinct provinces: particularly, at this time, he instituted the Privy Seal, which, besides its being appended to many of the writs that were ordained to pass under the seal formerly in use, which now, by way of distinction, came to be known by the name of the Great Seal, and to which the Privy Seal became, as it were, a preparatory step, it was appointed to give sufficient sanction of itself to several writs, which were not to pass any other seal. And it came at length to be an established rule, which is held to this day, that the rights of such things as might be conveyed among private persons by assignations, as rents, casualties, or other personal estate, were to pass by grants from the king under his Privy Seal alone; but those of lands and heritages, which among subjects are transmitted by dispositions, were to pass by grants from the king under the Great Seal. Accordingly the writs in use to pass under the Privy Seal alone, were gifts of offices, pensions, presentations to benefices, gifts of escheat, ward, marriage and relief, bastardy, *ultimus hæres*, and such like.

But as most of the writs which were to pass under the Great Seal were first to pass the Privy Seal, that afforded greater opportunity to examine the king's writs, and to prevent his majesty or his subjects from being hurt by obreption and fraud.

XIV.—Of the Lord Clerk-Register.

The Clerk-Register was of old the principal clerk in the kingdom, from whom all other clerks, who were his deputes, derived their immediate authority, and he himself acted as clerk to the parliament and council. He was called *Clericus rotulorum*, because of old the proceedings of parliament, and minutes and interlocutors of other courts, were not wrote in books, but in rolls of paper; hence they were termed *rotuli parliamenti*, the rolls of court; but thereafter they were appointed to be put in register-books, and the respective clerks ordained to transmit these books to the Clerk-Register to be preserved in the public archives or register. Whence his name of *Custos rotulorum*, which often occurs. By the treaty of union the preservation of the registers, in the same manner, is particularly provided for; and the return of the election of the sixteen Scots Peers to the British Parliament is ordered to be made by the Clerk-Register, or by two clerks of session, commissioned by him for that purpose.

XV.—Of the King's Advocate.

This is the same office with the *Advocatus fisci* among the Romans, and the Attorney-General in England; and his business is to pursue and defend in all causes wherein the king has an interest. His office was very honourable among the Romans, and he was dignified with the titles of *Clarissimus* and *Spectabilis*, which were bestowed only on the chief nobility; from whence probably it comes, that among the French he is designed *Messire*, which title is only bestowed on the Chancellor and Advocate, and that among us he is called *my Lord;* which, as a learned antiquarian observes, he found first given him in 1598.

His privileges are very extensive among us: for he is, as in France, *Consiliarius natus*, that is, a privy counsellor in a more particular way than the rest. He is allowed to sit within the bar of the court of session covered, where only the nobility are allowed to sit. And Sir George Mackenzie observes, he was allowed to be present at the Lords advising of causes wherein he himself was interested, which was introduced in Sir Thomas Hope's time. He issues warrants for apprehending and imprisoning, which are as valid as if granted by a judge. And as it was decided in the parliament of Paris in 1685, that the King's Advocate might at the same time be a judge, so with us Sir William Oliphant and Sir John Nisbet were both Advocates and Lords of Session at the same time.

THE STAGGERING STATE OF SCOTTISH STATESMEN.

CHANCELLORS.

1. James, Earl of *Morton*, Chancellor in Queen Mary's time, whose actions are at length set down in the histories of Buchanan and Knox, and Home's history of the family of Douglas, begot divers bastards, one of whom he made Laird of Spot, another Laird of Tofts. The first was purchased from his heirs by Sir Robert Douglas, and the last by one Belsches, an advocate. He was thereafter made regent in King James the VI.'s minority, *anno* 1572; but in that time was taxed with great avarice and extortion of the people, and by heightening the rate of money, and for coining of base coin, for adultery, and for delivering up the Earl of Northumberland to Queen Elizabeth, when he had fled to Scotland for refuge, being allured thereto by a sum of money.* He was overthrown by the means of the Earls of Argyle, Athole, and Montrose; and was accused and condemned for being art and part in the king's father's murder, which was proven by the means of Sir James Balfour, Clerk-Register, who produced his handwriting.

He got a response to beware of the Earl of Arran, which he conceived to be the Hamiltons, and therefore was their perpetual enemy; but in this he was mistaken, seeing, by the furiosity of the Earl of Arran, Captain James Stewart was made his guardian, and afterwards became Earl of Arran, and by his moyen† Morton was condemned, and his head taken off at the market-cross of Edinburgh. He caused to bring home that heading instrument called *The Maiden*, out of Halifax in Yorkshire, wherewith he was first himself beheaded, 2nd June, 1581.‡

---

* "The Earl of Northumberland had been delivered by the Earl of Mar, who was regent before Morton."—*Goodal.*

† Unlawful means.

‡ It was "The Gibbet Law" of Halifax, that a felon who had stolen goods within the liberty of the place should be taken to the gibbet, and have his head

2. George, Earl of *Huntly*, chancellor in the time of Henry and Mary.* He was father to George, the first Marquis of Huntly, who slew the Earl of Murray, and burnt his house of Dunnybirsle, and did many other cruel actions, set down in Mr. Melvil's verses; † and grandfather to George, late Marquis of Huntly, who, for assisting James Graham, the Marquis of Montrose, in the late troubles, against this kingdom, being apprehended and brought to Edinburgh, had his head struck off in 1648.‡ His whole lands were apprised for debts, and most part of them are now in the hands of his brother-in-law, the Marquis of Argyle. His second brother, the Lord

---

cut off. The execution took place on the market-day, in order to strike terror, and was performed by means of an instrument called a gibbet, which was raised upon a platform, four feet high, and thirteen feet square, faced on each side with stone, and ascended by a flight of steps. In the middle of this platform were placed two upright pieces of timber, fifteen feet high, joined at the top by a tranverse beam. Within these was a square block of wood, four feet and a half long, which moved up and down by means of grooves made for that purpose, to the lower part of which was fastened an iron axe, which weighed seven pounds and twelve ounces. The axe thus fixed was drawn up by means of a cord and pulley. At the head of the cord was a pin, fixed to the block, which kept it suspended till the moment of execution, when the culprit's head being placed on the block, the pin was withdrawn, and his head severed from his body. In passing through Halifax, the Regent Morton witnessed one of these executions. He ordered a model to be made of the gibbet, and, on his return to Scotland, had a similar ininstrument constructed, which, remaining long unused, was called "The Maiden." The instrument is now in the museum of the Society of Antiquaries at Edinburgh. —*Halifax Gibbet and Gibbet Law.* By John Ryley Robinson, LL.D., Stokesley, 1871, 12mo.

* George, fifth Earl of Huntly, was appointed Chancellor 20th March, 1565. He died suddenly, May, 1576.

† The verses referred to were doubtless written by Andrew or James Melville, the eminent Presbyterian divines, both of whom composed verses—the former in Latin, the latter in his native tongue (James Melville's Autobiography, &c., Edin., 1842, 8vo., pp. xlv.—xlvii.). The slaughter of "the bonny Earl of Murray" by the Marquis of Huntly, forms the subject of two old ballads (Maidment's "Scottish Ballads and Songs," Edin. 1818, 8vo., vol. i., pp. 234—9). James, fourth Earl of Murray, was slain in his house at Dunibristle, Fifeshire, in February, 1592.

‡ The author errs in describing the second Marquis of Huntly as having assisted the Marquis of Montrose. Huntly, who had by Charles I. been appointed his lieutenant-general in the north, was jealous of Montrose, who held office as lieutenant-general of the kingdom; besides he had some private wrongs to avenge. He therefore declined to co-operate with him—a resolution which proved fatal to the king, to Montrose, and to himself. Huntly was beheaded on the 22nd March, 1649.

Aboyne,* and other four with him, as by divine providence revenging the fact of Dunnybirsle, were, in 1630, with a sudden fire in the night, burnt quick in the house of Frendraught.

The Lord Gordon,† eldest son to the last marquis, was shot dead at a field with James Graham; so that family is very near extinct and going to decay.

3. John Lyon, Lord *Glammis*, was made chancellor in King James's minority, 24th October, 1573. He was a good justiciar, but bruiked ‡ the place only a few years; for, on the 17th March, 1577, he was shot at Stirling with a bullet by the Earl of Crawford and his followers, for a controversy that fell out betwixt them anent their marches. His grandchild, the late lord, died of the plague of pestilence, leaving behind him such a burden of debt upon the estate, that it behoved his mother to procure a warrant from the lords to sell lands till all the debts were paid.

4. John, Earl of *Athole*, was made chancellor after Glammis, but lived in the place but few years; yet in his time he did great oppressions to many, that he might augment his estate and grandeur, whereof this was not the least, that at the instigation of his mother he killed Sir John Rattray of that Ilk, being about the ninetieth year of his age, while he was sitting praying in his own chapel, by James Stewart, one of his domestics; who having but two daughters, Grizel and Jean Rattray, procreate on dame Elizabeth Kennedy, daughter to the Earl of Cassilis, he married the eldest himself, and

* Sir John Gordon, second son of the Marquis of Huntly, was by Charles I. in 1627 created Viscount Melgum and Lord Aboyne; he perished with Gordon of Rothiemay and their six attendants in the burning of the house of Frendraught on the 18th October, 1630. The event has been commemorated in a pathetic ballad. For this composition, as well as an intelligent account of the burning of Frendraught Castle, see Maidment's "Scottish Ballads," Edin., 1868, 8vo., vol. i., pp. 262—271.

† George, Lord Gordon, eldest son of the second Marquis of Huntly, fell at the battle of Alford on the 2nd July, 1645. He was deeply lamented by Montrose and his army. On account of having composed a few lines "on black eyes," included in Watson's Collection, Part III., his name has obtained a place in Walpole's "Catalogue of Royal and Noble Authors."

‡ *Angl.* "enjoyed." Lord Glammis corresponded with Theodore Beza, the colleague of Calvin, on the subject of church polity. After his death Andrew Melville bestowed on him the following epigram:—

"Tu leo magne jaces inglorius; ergo manebunt
    Qualia fata canes? qualia fata sues?"

gave the other to Sir James Stewart of Balvenie, his brother. By this marriage he joined to his own estate the baronies of Rattray and Redcastle; so that by that cruel fact, none was left of that house but a brother called *Sylvester*, who, being also pursued for his life, was preserved by flying to a room of his own, called Craighall, which he possesses to this day. He was poisoned by means of the Earl of Morton, and died at Kincardine, 24th April, 1579;* and albeit at his death he left his estate flourishing, yet did his successor sell the same wholly to the Murrays of Tullibardine and others; and two of the sons of the house have wandered the country these forty years begging.

5. Colin, Earl of *Argyle*, succeeded to be chancellor after Athole, who also continued not long in the office. His house found little advantage, but hurt thereby; for there was so great burden of debt upon the same, that it behoved his son, the late earl, to leave the country, not being able to give satisfaction to his creditors. He went over to West Flanders to serve the King of Spain, and became a papist, of whose flight the poet Craig † wrote these lines,—

"Now Earl of Guile and Lord Forlorn thou goes,
Quitting thy prince to serve his Spanish foes.
No faith in plaids, no trust in highland trews,
Camelion-like, they change so many hues."

---

* John, fourth Earl of Athole, was elected Chancellor 29th March, 1577 (Privy Council Records). His father, the third earl, married as his first wife, Grizel, daughter of Sir John Rattray, of that ilk. Sir John had married Elizabeth, daughter of John, second Lord Kennedy, by whom he had, besides the daughters mentioned in the text, three sons. The eldest son predeceased him, without issue. On that event, Athole maintained his right to share in the succession proportionately with Sir John's two surviving sons. To insure his claim, he took possession of Rattray Castle, and plundered the family papers. Patrick Rattray, the lawful heir, took refuge in the Castle of Craighall. On the death of Patrick, Sylvester, the surviving brother, was unable to effect his service as heir at Perth, the county town, on account of the hostilities of Lord Athole and his friends. The service was therefore performed at Dundee ('Douglas' Baronage,' 276—7). The story of the slaughter of Sir John Rattray by the Earl of Athole is totally unsupported. It is evidently one of those calumnies which our author was only too prone to credit and record. Nor was the Earl poisoned through the instrumentality of the Regent Morton. He died a few days after dining with the regent at Stirling Castle. But a *post mortem* examination showed that he died from natural causes.—*Crawfura's Officers of State*, Edin., 1726, folio, p. 135.

† Alexander Craig published "Poeticall Essayes," London, 1604, 4to.; and "Poetical Recreations," Edinburgh, 1609, 4to. He has contributed to the "Muses

He gave to his son of the second marriage the lordship of Kintyre, which he sold in a few years to his brother, and went to the French wars, where he died.

His heir, Archibald, now Marquis of Argyle, being well educated, was early made a councillor, and created marquis in 1633.* At that time there was great appearance of an alliance to have been made betwixt his son and the Marquis of Hamilton's daughter; and they two together fled from the parliament, having information that some plot was laid for their destruction; yet, some few days thereafter, things being pacified, they returned and sat again in parliament. But since that time their sweetest wine became their sourest vinegar; for an inveterate hatred has ever been betwixt them, and by their factions this kingdom has become a prey and conquest to the English nation.

6. Captain James Stewart,† thereafter styled Earl of Arran, was

---

Welcome," and was also author of a volume entitled "The Amorous Songs, Sonnets, and Elegies of Mr. Alexander Craig, Scoto-Briton.," Lond., 1606, 12mo. In 1605 he received a pension, which was two years afterwards ratified by an Act of the Scottish Parliament. A person of his name was Commissioner for Banff in the parliament of 1621.

* Colin, sixth Earl of Argyle, was appointed Chancellor 16th August, 1579. He died in 1584. His son Archibald, seventh earl, was a brave officer, and was some time connected with the Spanish service. That he became papist rests on the insufficient authority of our too credulous author. The grandson of Colin, sixth earl, was the famous Marquis of Argyle who was beheaded 27th May, 1661.

† In the more modern copies, the account of the Chancellor Arran is presented in these words:—

"James Stewart, son to the Lord Ochiltree. His rising and advancement was by his accusation of the Earl of Morton of treason in face of the council, as being art and part of King James VI.'s father's murder, after whose execution he was exalted in credit by the king, then being seventeen years, or thereby, and made captain of his guards by the Earl of Arran, and a counsellor, so that nothing was done in state, council and session, without his special order and direction. By him Sir John Maitland had first favour with the king; and his lady, being of the house of Lovat, called him oftentimes her man Maitland; neither was there any causes called in the outer-house of the session, but by such tickets as were reached out of her hand to the lord there sitting; so that he grew so insolent thereby, that he pretended to have right to the crown, as nearest kinsman to Duke Murdo; and the king was very glad, when he publicly in the session renounced, and quit-claimed whatsomever title he could pretend to the crown, and, casting in a crown of the sun, took instrument thereof in the clerk Robert Scot's hands. His lady, being curious to chancellor to King James, and ruled all at his pleasure; and his lady, Elizabeth Stewart, daughter to the Earl of Athole, was accustomed to sit in the session on the bench beside the lord of the outer-house, who called no tickets of causes but by her order. She styled Mr. Maitland, thereafter chancellor, her man Maitland. She was divorced from her first husband, the Earl of March, for his alleged impotency; so that Arran was in one day husband to her, and father to her child, as Johnston* says in his story.

---

know the estate of her family, advised with witches, and got this response, that her husband should be the highest head in Scotland, and she the greatest woman in it. Both which fell out contrary to their mind; for she died of the hydropsy, and a great swelling of her body; and he, after a short space, being made chancellor in 1584, as riding through Crawfordmuir, was invaded by the Lord Torthorald and his son, and there slain, his head separate from his body, and carried upon the point of a lance, in revenge of Morton's death. He had a son called Sir James, who also was Lord Ochiltree, and had little better success than his father: who albeit he lived to a great age, and had great accession to the estate by the living of Salton, concredited to him, as was averred, in trust; yet he sold the same totally for his own behoof, and defrauded the righteous heir of the same. And after he had, in imitation of his father, accused Sir Gideon Murray, then treasurer-depute, of misguiding the king's rents, which was the occasion of his death, by starving himself to death divers years thereafter; he accused also James, Duke of Hamilton, of high treason, avowing to prove that he aimed at the crown; but the Duke having greater credit with the king, found moyen that he was misbelieved, and got him sent home from London, prisoner, to the castle of Blackness, where he lived sundry years upon the king's expense, till the change of government, 1652; at which time being enlarged by the English, and falling short of means, he behoved to betake himself to be a physician (which art he had studied in prison), whereby he sustained himself and family till his death, and apparently will never have a successor, none of his lands being to the fore."

Captain Stewart, Earl of Arran, was second son of Andrew, Lord Ochiltree, a zealous promoter of the Reformation. He was an unworthy favourite of James VI., who gave him all the power of the government; in 1584 he was constituted chancellor and lieutenant of the kingdom. In 1585 he was degraded from his honours and banished from court. In 1596 he was encountered and slain by James Douglas of Parkhead, nephew of the regent Morton, in revenge for his having caused the regent's death, by accusing him of being accessory to the murder of Darnley. (Crawfurd's "Officers of State").

* Robert Johnston, author of "Historia Rerum Britannicarum," &c., from 1572 to 1628, published at Amsterdam in 1655, and of "The History of Scotland during the minority of James VI.," published at London in 1646. A MS. history of Scotland, preserved in the Advocates Library, is supposed to have been partly written by Johnston. He died about 1630.

One day in the session, King James being present, the said captain James took a French crown out of his pocket and cast to the clerk, taking therewith instruments, that he claimed no right to the crown, albeit he said he was descended of Duke Murdo; wherewith it is said the king was as well pleased as if he had received from him the greatest favour in the world.

He was brought in by Esme, Duke of Lennox. His lady got a response from the witches, that she should be the greatest woman in Scotland, and that her husband should have the highest head in that kingdom; both which fell out; for she died, being all swelled in an extraordinary manner; and he, riding to the south, was pursued by the Lord Torthorald (called Douglas), whose whole family the said Captain James intended to have extirpated, and was killed, and his head carried on the point of a spear till it was brought to a church-yard. After which time the Hamiltons were restored to their own estate of Arran.

His son James attained to the title of Lord Ochiltree, but enjoyed the estate few years, and was forced to sell all for defraying of his debts.

He it was that accused James, marquis of Hamilton, of treason; but because either he could not clear the matter sufficiently, or because the king would not believe a misreport of a man whom he so much loved, he was sent prisoner to Blackness, and lay there ten or twelve years. In the end being dismissed, he has taken himself to be a doctor of medicine, by which means he sustains himself and his family.*

7. Mr. John Maitland, second brother to secretary Maitland, after he had studied law in France, was preferred to be a lord of session by means of the Earl of Arran, and thereafter became chancellor. He was one of the Octavians,† and was created Lord Thirlestane, and was an excellent Latin poet, as his verses inserted in *Delitiæ Poetarum Scotorum* testify; and King James had such a respect to him, that he made the epitaph engraven on his tomb.‡ Yet

* Sir James Stewart, of Killeth, who succeeded as fifth Lord Ochiltree, and whose unworthy career is set forth in the text, died in 1659. He was succeeded by his grandson William, sixth Lord Ochiltree, who died unmarried in 1675, when the title became extinct. "Douglas's Peerage," Edin., 1764, fol., pp. 523-4.

† The Octavians were the eight financial advisers of James VI.; they were so called from their number.

‡ Chancellor Maitland was second son of Sir Richard Maitland of Lethington, the poet, and was born in 1537. He became chancellor in 1586, and was created Lord Thirlestane in 1589. He died 3rd October, 1595. The epitaph composed

the conquest he made of the barony of Liddington from his brother's son, James Maitland, was not thought lawful nor conscientious.

He left behind him a son and daughter. The son having married chancellor Seton's daughter by dame Jean Fleming, and aiming at his father's place, by his moyen was made a lord of session ; which place he enjoyed all King James's time, till in King Charles's time he was displaced with the rest of the noblemen.* His daughter was married to the Lord Seton, who, the first night, became mad and threw a chamber-pot in her bosom, and was imprisoned in Seton, and his brother got the earldom.

His grandson, now Earl of Lauderdale,† married one of the heiresses of Home, hoping to have got a half of that estate ; but was disappointed thereof by the heir of tailzie, who was preferred to him by a sentence of law. He was one of the commissioners from the General Assembly to England ; but being among those who plotted the relief of the king at Scarborough Castle in England, he was

---

for him by James VI. was engraved on a marble tablet attached to his monument in the parish church of Haddington. It was as follows :—

    HAEC JACOBUS REX SEXTUS.

  Thou passenger, who spiest with gazing eyes
    This sad trophy of death's triumphant dart,
  Consider, when this outward tomb thou sees,
    How rare a man leaves here his earthly part ;
  His wisdom and his uprightness of heart,
    His piety, his practice in our state,
  His pregnant wit, well-versed in every part,
    As equally not all were in debate.
  Then justly hath his death brought forth, of late,
    A heavy grief to prince and subjects all,
  Who virtue love, and vice do truly hate,
    Though vicious men be joyful at his fall ;
  But for himself, most happy doth he die,
    Though for his prince it most unhappy be."

* The son of Chancellor Maitland was created Earl of Lauderdale in 1624, and in 1644 was elected president of the Estates of Parliament. He died on the 20th January, 1645, and by William Drummond of Hawthornden, the poet, was commemorated in a Latin elegy.

† John, second Earl, and afterwards Duke of Lauderdale, was born at Lethington on the 21st May, 1616. A zealous Presbyterian, he was in 1643 appointed one of the commissioners from the Church of Scotland to the Westminster Assembly. He afterwards withdrew from the Presbyterian cause, and joined the court of Charles II. at the Hague. On the Restoration he was relieved from imprison-

declared an enemy to the State, and debarred from returning until the king's coming home, in 1650. Then he was brought home and convoyed the king to that last expedition against England; where being taken at the field of Worcester, he was carried up to London and imprisoned in the Tower, where he lies at this present. And albeit his estate was great, by the conquests of his grandfather and father, yet it is well known at this day, that if all men were paid their lawful debts, there would be little or nothing left thereof.

8. John, Earl of Montrose, succeeded as chancellor in the place of the said Lord Thirlestane, in whose time that line was written in the sederunt house—

"Et bibulo memini consule nil fieri,"

for he was altogether void of learning; which King James finding, and perceiving his error, got a fair means to shuffle him out, by making him viceroy at a parliament in 1604, and putting in Chancellor Seton in his place; after which he retired home.*

His son bruiked his estate, but lived at home, till in his old age he was made President of the Council, in July, 1626, a year before his death.

His grandson, James, Earl of Montrose, is so well known in these times, that there needs not much to be written here concerning him; only this, that his mother consulted with witches at his birth; and that his father said to a gentleman who was sent to visit him from a neighbour earl, that that child would trouble all Scotland. He is said also to have eaten a toad whilst he was a sucking child. He was divers years very zealous for the Covenant; and at the first time when the English came down to the Bricks,† when the Scots army lay at Dunselaw, the lot of his regiment was first to cross the Tweed,

---

ment in the Tower, and appointed Secretary of State for Scotland. In 1664 he sanctioned the erection of the Court of High Commission, a tribunal intended for the subversion of the Scottish Presbyterian Church. In 1674 the House of Commons petitioned the king to remove him from State employment. He died at Tunbridge Wells on the 24th August, 1682.

* John, third Earl of Montrose, was Chancellor of the Jury at the trial of the Regent Morton. In January, 1597, he was appointed Chancellor of the kingdom: he demitted the office in 1604, when, with a pension of £2,000 Scots, he was constituted Viceroy of Scotland. In this capacity he presided in the parliament held at Perth on the 9th July, 1606, when episcopal government was thrust upon the Church. He died on the 9th November, 1608, in his sixty-first year.

John, fourth Earl of Montrose, was appointed President of the Council in July, 1626, and died on the 26th of November following.

† Within three miles from Berwick-on-Tweed.

which he did himself in the midst of winter, boots and all. Yet thereafter, at subscribing the League and Covenant, finding that General Leslie was preferred to him, he changed his mind and took him to the king's party; and took a commission from his majesty to reduce Scotland to his obedience. And having the assistance of three or four hundred Irishmen, under the conduct of Alaster Macdonald, he defeated the Scots forces six times, and killed in these above eighteen regiments, as he says in his book. The places where these fields were, are Tippermuir, Aberdeen, Alford, Auldern, Innerlochie, and Kilsyth. Yet was he beaten, fifteen days after the last fight of Kilsyth, by David Leslie, lieutenant-general of the Scots army, at Philiphaugh. After that by capitulation, he was sent out of the kingdom; and, in King Charles the Second's time, having got his commission renewed, and coming to Ross with his forces, expecting to have got much assistance, was there beaten by three troops of Colonel Strachan's, and himself taken prisoner and brought to Edinburgh, and hanged at the market-cross, his head taken off, his body parted in four, his quarters sent to sundry towns of the kingdom, and his head put upon the Tolbooth of Edinburgh. His estate was shared amongst his friends after his forfeiture for relief of his cautioners, and the burdens which they had undertaken for him.*

9. Sir Alexander Seton, thereafter styled Earl of Dunfermline, was made chancellor in King James VI.'s time, and possessed the same place the space of twenty years, and was one of the Octavians. In his youth he lived divers years in Italy, and is said to have received orders of priesthood in Rome; and that his chalice, wherewith he said mass, at his home-coming was sold in Edinburgh. He was a son of the house of Seton, and had his preferment by Queen Anne. He was first an ordinary Lord of Session, and styled prior of Pluscardie. He thereafter conquest many lordships, viz., the earldom of

* The celebrated James Graham, first Marquis of Montrose, was born in 1612. At first a zealous upholder of Presbyterianism, he supported the cause by arms; he subsequently attached himself to Charles I., by whom he was appointed Lieutenant-General of the kingdom. His fame as a military leader rests on his successes against the Covenanters in six engagements, commencing with the battle of Tippermuir, fought on the 1st September, 1644, and terminating with his victory at Kilsyth on the 15th August, 1645. He was defeated by General Leslie at Philiphaugh on the 13th September, 1643, and on an attempt to restore the authority of the exiled king, he was, on the 27th April, 1650, surprised and routed by Colonel Strachan at Invercharron, Ross-shire. Having been delivered into the hands of General Leslie, he was conveyed to Edinburgh, where he was executed on the 21st May, 1650.

Dunfermline, by the king's gift, the lordship of Urquhart, the baronies of Fyvie, Delgaty, and Pinkie. He professed himself a Protestant in outward show, but died an avowed Papist.*

He married his four daughters, one to the Earl of Lauderdale, one to the Earl of Seaforth, one to the Earl of Kellie, and one to the Lord Balcarras; all which families except the last are gone to ruin.

He left his only son, Charles, Earl of Dunfermline, in a flourishing estate; but in a few years after his majority, by playing, and other inordinate spending, all was comprised from him; and when he was debarred by promise to play at no game, he devised a new way to elude his oath, by wagering with any who was in his company who should draw the longest straw out of a stack with the most grains of corn thereon. He got a vast gift from King Charles, viz., a three nineteen years tack of the abbacy of Dunfermline, which is worth in yearly rent £20,000, and in that space, if he shall happen to bruik it, it will amount to 1,100,000 merks. † The said lord chancellor ‡ was a good humanist and a poet, as testifies that epigram prefixed to Leslie's chronicle of Scotland—

"Siccine vos titulis tantum gaudetis avorum,
 Nec pudet antiquam descruisse fidem.
At titulos dedit alma fides, dedit inclita virtus;
 Has nostri semper nam coluere patres.

---

* Sir Alexander Seton, first Earl of Dunfermline, was third son of George, sixth Lord Seton, and was born about the year 1555. Being intended for the Church, he went to Rome and became a student in the College of Jesuits. The downfall of the Romish Church in Scotland induced him to abandon ecclesiastical for legal studies. Having passed advocate, he was by James VI. in 1583 appointed an Extraordinary Lord of Session; in 1593 he was elected President of the Court. After holding various other offices, he was elevated to the Chancellorship in 1604: he was created Earl of Dunfermline in 1606. In 1609 he was admitted a member of the English Privy Council. He died at his seat, Pinkie House, near Edinburgh, on the 16th June, 1622. He is commended in their histories both by Spottiswood and Calderwood, the latter asserting that he was "nae good friend to the bishops."

† Charles, second Earl of Dunfermline, was a zealous adherent of the Covenant, and was employed by the Estates in several important negotiations with Charles I. He supported the "Engagement" in 1648, and in the following year visited Charles II. on the Continent, returning with him to Scotland in 1650. At the Restoration he was sworn a Privy Councillor, and was appointed Lord Privy Seal in 1671. He died in 1673.

‡ The chancellor is celebrated as a scholar by Arthur Johnston in one of his panegyrics. He addressed an epigram to Sir John Skene on his publication of the *Regiam Majestatem*.

Cernitis, his modo desertis, ut gloria nostra
Conciderit, gentis conciderit que decus.
Ergo est priscorum pietas repetenda parentum,
Ut referat nobis secula prisca Deus."

10. Sir George Hay of Nethercliff, who before was clerk-register, was made chancellor after Dunfermline. He was son to the bailie of Errol, laird of Megginch, and being bred at Douay with his uncle, Mr. Edmund Hay, a Jesuit, came over to England, and attended the Earl of Carlisle there, by whom he was preferred to be a gentleman-pensioner, and thereafter to be a gentleman of the privy-chamber. After that, by moyen of the Popish faction in England, he was advanced to the said dignity of state, hoping that way to have him their friend when they should be troubled for religion, being in that kingdom. He had little or no learning; yet did he conquest a good estate, and procured the same to be erected by his majesty into an earldom, viz., the baronies of Kinnoul, Aberdalgy, Dupplin, Kinfauns, Seggieden, Dunninald, and many others;* all which estates, in a few years after his decease, his son made havoc of.†

His only daughter he married to the Lord Spynie,‡ a noble spendthrift and exquisite in all manner of debauchery, to whom she bore three sons; the eldest married the Earl of Ethie's daughter, but impotent altogether for a woman, as was known after his death; the second was drowned; and the third was taken prisoner in England at the battle of Worcester. His own lady caused put him in prison

* Sir George Hay was second son of Peter Hay of Megginch. Born in 1572, he was educated at the Scots college of Douay under his uncle Edmund, well known as Father Hay. In 1596 he was introduced at court by his relative, Sir James Hay of Kingask, and was appointed a Gentleman of the Bedchamber. After holding a succession of offices he was at length elevated to the chancellorship on the 16th January, 1622. He was created Earl of Kinnoul by patent dated 25th May, 1633. He died at London on the 16th December, 1634, and was interred in the parish church of Kinnoul, where an elegant monument, with his statue habited in his chancellor's robes, was erected to his memory. He is commemorated by Arthur Johnston in a Latin epitaph.

† George Hay, second Earl of Kinnoul, was a faithful adherent of Charles I.; he refused to subscribe the Solemn League and Covenant. He died on the 5th October, 1644.

‡ Alexander Lindsay, second Lord Spynie, fought in Germany under Gustavus Adolphus of Sweden. He was appointed muster-master-general in 1626. After the battle of Tippermuir he joined the Marquis of Montrose in September, 1644; he was on the 19th of that month taken prisoner at Aberdeen by the Earl of Argyle. He died in March, 1656.

at Dundee for his debauchery, where he died miserably. So that the whole estate of Spynie is for the most part disponed and gone. And of the said earl and his family may be said that verse which Chancellor Maitland made of another courtier in his time :—

"Absque modo intumuit, ceciditque ut bulla superbus,
    Et redit in nihilum, qui fuit ante nihil."

11. Mr. John Spottiswood,* parson of Calder, was son of Mr. John Spottiswood, superintendant of Lothian, in the time of the reformation of religion. He was made a bishop when the other eleven a year or two after King James's going to England were restored to their dignities. He was made Archbishop of Glasgow in the parliament 1606; and, at the death of Mr. George Gladstanes, Archbishop of St. Andrews, succeeded to him in that place.

* John Spottiswood, Archbishop of St. Andrews, was eldest son of John Spottiswood, superintendant of Lothian; he was born in 1565. Having studied at the University of Glasgow, he was in his eighteenth year ordained minister of Calder. While in England attending James VI. in 1603 he was appointed Archbishop of Glasgow. In 1606 he was summoned by the king to the celebrated conference at Hampton Court. In 1615 he was advanced to the Archbishopric of St. Andrews and the primacy. He was a sincere upholder of episcopacy, and was the means of passing the five articles in the General Assembly at Perth in 1618. He was appointed Chancellor in 1635. On the introduction of the Service-book in 1637, he gave his countenance to the project, and consequently became obnoxious. He was charged with numerous offences, and excommunicated by the Assembly of 1638. He retired to Newcastle, and being in feeble health, renounced the office of chancellor. Proceeding to London, he was seized with fever, and there died on the 24th November, 1639. His remains were interred in Westminster Abbey, where a marble monument (long since removed) was erected to his memory. It bore these lines:—

"Præsul, Senator, pene Martyr hic jacet
Quo nemo Sanctior, Gravior, Constantior,
Pro Ecclesia, pro Rege, pro Recta Fide,
Contra Sacrileges, Perduelles, Perfidos,
Stetit ad extremum usque Vitæ Spiritum,
Solitamque talium Meritorum Præmium,
Diras Rapinas Exiliumque pertulit,
Sed hac in Urna, in Ore Postremum, in Deo
Victor potitur Pace, Fama, Gloria."

(Crawfurd's "Officers of State," p. 193). Archbishop Spottiswood composed a "History of the Church and State of Scotland," a work alike creditable to his learning and impartiality.

He was greatly blotted by the public fame* both of drunkenness and licentiousness, as that verse made on him testifies:—

"Vinum amat Andreas, cum vino Glasgoa amores."

He was made chancellor after the death of Kinnoul; but, before he had possessed the place two years, for bringing in the Service-book he was expelled the kingdom, and forced to fly to England, where he died in 1639.

In the year 1606 he caused imprison five or six of the ministry for holding a General Assembly at Aberdeen, being discharged by the king, and indicted them of their lives in Linlithgow, and banished them the kingdom. The men were Mr. Andrew and James Melvill, Mr. Andrew Duncan, Mr. Robert Durie, Mr. John Forbes, Mr. John Carmichael, and Mr. John Welsh; at which time the said Mr. John Welsh wrote two letters, one to the laird of Kilsyth, and another to the lady Fleming, clearly telling and prophesying of the blood that should be shed in Scotland for contempt of the gospel, and of the decay of that bishop and his posterity.

He had two sons, Sir John and Sir Robert. To the eldest he conquest the lairdship of Dairsie and Kincaple, being worth £500 sterling per annum. The other he procured to be made president of the session, who indeed was an able scholar, and noways, to the sight of the world, evil inclined; only he followed his father's way, and left the kingdom. Of his end we shall speak hereafter in his life.† Sir John sold the whole lands. He had married Sir William Irving's daughter, who also purchased the barony of Kelly, being fourscore chalders of victual, which also he behoved to sell again, and there is nothing left thereof. Sir Robert, before his death, sold the baronies of Whitekirk to George Home, of Foord, and the barony of Duni-pace to Mr. James Aikenhead; both of which he had conquest himself by assistance of his father a few years ago. So that the said Mr. John Welsh's prophecy is very likely to take effect. He had but one

---

* The private character of the Archbishop was untainted, but he temporarily suffered from the calumnies of his ecclesiastical opponents. Of these, the most uncompromising was Andrew Melville, the famous Presbyterian divine, who, it is believed, composed the line of Latin verse which our author has been at too great pains to preserve.

† See *Postea*, under "Secretaries of State."

daughter, married to the laird of Roslin,* which family is utterly gone, being the principal house of old of the earls of Caithness.

12. John Campbell, son to the laird of Lawers, who married the heretrix of Loudoun, for his learning was made choice of by the king and parliament to be chancellor. He was created earl in 1633, and was much respected for his sincere profession of religion. But *honores mutant mores;* for being sent to the king from the parliament he was imprisoned in the Tower, and ran a great risk of his life; for there was a warrant sent to Sir William Balfour, lieutenant of the Tower, to behead him. But Sir William procured a countermand by the Marquis of Hamilton's moyen, and so preserved his life: for which cause the chancellor undertook to raise an army in Scotland to assist the king, and by the Duke of Hamilton's faction was chosen, at the parliament of 1648, president of that parliament wherein the engagement was concluded. And for all that, thereafter the commissioners of the kirk, upon his repentance and acknowledgment of his fault, made him to be restored to his former estimation.

He was blotted of incontinence, whether justly or not his own conscience best knows; and was thereafter accused before the Presbystery for lying with the wife of one Johnston, a major of the army; but the matter could not be cleared at that time, both because the English army was then near the border, and the Presbytery were greatly his friends, for the help they had got from him in the augmentation of their stipends.

He bought the annuities due to the king from James Livingston, and thereby got a huge deal of money from the nobility and gentry for selling each one their own, with which he intended to buy Cumnock barony; but the troubles stopped that bargain, and he behoved to fly to his native country, the Highlands, and is thought to have taken the money with him. In the meantime, his place was declared void by the English, as all the rest of the places were which depended on the crown. His whole estate and lands were many times comprised for debts, and first by the lady of James Livingston, from whom he bought the right of annuities.†

---

* It was Anne, only daughter of the archbishop, who married Sir William St. Clair of Roslin, representative of an opulent and distinguished House. Sir John errs both in describing the gentlewoman's parentage and also the condition of her husband's estate. Roslin remained in the family of the St. Clairs till 1736.

† Sir John Campbell, afterwards Earl of Loudoun, was eldest son of Sir James

TREASURERS.

1. John Hamilton, Archbishop of St. Andrews, and base son to the Earl of Arran, was treasurer when George, Earl of Huntly, was chancellor in the queen's time.*

He was blotted as being accessory to the murder of the king committed by the Earl of Bothwell, and, that night it was committed, was marked to lodge in his brother's house, which now is the college of Edinburgh, hard by the kirk of Field, where the murder was perpetrated. He also did instigate the Barons of the Border to invade England, when Queen Mary was put in close prison, *anno*

Campbell, of Lawers, of the family of Glenurchy. In 1620 he married Margaret Campbell, Baroness of Loudoun, and in consequence was styled Lord Loudoun. He was created Earl of Loudoun, in May, 1633, but owing to his opposition to Court measures, his patent was suspended for eight years. He resisted the unconstitutional attempt of Charles I. to force episcopacy on the nation in 1637; he was an active member of the General Assembly of 1638, and in 1639 he garrisoned for the Covenanters the castles of Strathaven, Douglas, and Tantallon. He was one of the commissioners who settled the pacification at Berwick. In 1640, having proceeded to London as commissioner from the Committee of the Estates, he was arrested on a charge of treason and committed to the Tower; he regained his liberty through favour of the Marquis of Hamilton. In August 1640 he held command in the Scottish army at the battle of Newburn; he presided at the opening of the Estates in the July following. During the royal visit in 1641 he was appointed chancellor, and first commissioner of the Treasury. With two others he was sent to treat with the king in Carisbrooke Castle in 1647; he at first concurred in the "engagement," but afterwards withdrew from it. Soon after the defeat of Charles II. at Worcester, in 1651, he retired into private life. At the Restoration he was deprived of his chancellorship, and fined £12,000. He died on the 13th March, 1663. His morals have been impugned by our author only.

* John Hamilton was in 1625 appointed Abbot of Paisley; he was preferred to the bishopric of Dunkeld in 1643, and in the same year became successively keeper of the privy seal and treasurer of the kingdom. On the assassination of Cardinal Beaton, in May, 1546, he was elevated to the primacy as Archbishop of St. Andrews. He founded the Divinity College at St. Andrews for the better education of the clergy, but sternly opposed and persecuted the promoters of Reformation. After his capture at Dunbarton Castle on the 1st April, 1571, he was subjected to trial as an accomplice in the murder of Darnley, but proof having failed, he was, on the ground of being previously forfeited, condemned to death by the Regent Morton. He was hanged at Stirling Bridge in his pontifical robes on the 5th April, 1571. The archbishop led a somewhat dissolute life: he openly kept a mistress, who bore him several children.—(Crawfurd's Officers of State).

1567; but after the field of Langside, he fled to Dumbarton Castle, where, being apprehended, he, at command of the viceroy, the Earl of Lennox, was brought to Stirling, and there hanged; whereof one wrote these lines :—

> " Vive diu, felix arbor, semperque vireto
> Frondibus, ut nobis talia poma feras."

He left the lands of Blair, and others, to his base son, whose son John, after he had quitted his wife by playing the harlot by her, sold all the land, and fled the country; and these lands of Blair belong now to the laird of Fairney.*

2. Mr. Robert Richardson,† commendator of St. Mary's Isle, was treasurer to Queen Mary. He conquest a great estate. To his eldest son he gave the baronies of Smeton and Wallyford; and many lands about Musselburgh, with the mills thereof. To the second the barony of Pencaitland. The eldest, Sir James, disponed the mills of Musselburgh and divers lands to Lauderdale, and the rest of the lands about Inveresk to Chancellor Seton; but as yet his grandson brooks Smeton and Wallyford. But the son of Sir Robert, the second son, has sold all the barony of Pencaitland to Mr. James Macgill of Cranston-riddel.

3. William, Earl of Gowrie; he was, in all appearance, the son of the Lord Ruthven, ‡ who, in his old age, with the Lord Lindsay, at

* Archbishop Hamilton was succeeded as treasurer by Gilbert, Earl of Cassilis, who held office from 1554 till his death in 1558. Being one of the Scottish Commissioners who witnessed the marriage of the youthful Queen Mary to the Dauphin, he was asked to give consent that the Dauphin should assume the Scottish crown. With the other commissioners, he refused to acquiesce in this proposal. Not long after, with two of his colleagues, he died suddenly at Dieppe, on the 28th November, 1558, and there were grave suspicions that poison had been administered.—(Crawfurd's Officers of State).

† Richardson was an opulent burgess of Edinburgh, and being much reputed for his integrity, was appointed treasurer by the Queen Regent on the death of Lord Cassilis. He held the treasurership till his death in 1571.—(Crawfurd's Officers of State).

‡ He was eldest surviving son of the third Lord Ruthven. He took part in the murder of Rizzio, joined the association against the Earl of Bothwell in 1567, and as a commissioner, along with Lord Lindsay, announced Queen Mary's intention to renounce the government. On the 24th June, 1571, he was appointed treasurer for life. Long an attached friend of the Earl of Morton, he became his bitterest enemy, and was one of those who accelerated his death. He was created Earl of Gowrie on the 23rd August, 1581. He was instigator and chief actor in the Raid of Ruthven, 23rd August, 1582, for which he received the royal pardon in December,

the request of the king, killed Signor Davie, the Italian, in Queen Mary's bedchamber. After he had exercised the office of treasurer some years, and had brought a great debt on his family, he was in the end accused of treason, convicted thereof, and his head struck off in the town of Stirling, in King James VI.'s youth. Yet were his children by Dorothea Stuart, his lady, rehabilitate, being four, John, Alexander, William, and Patrick. John, in his youth, being well educated in the College of Edinburgh, travelled through France and Italy; and within a year after his return, he, with his brother, Mr. Alexander, were both killed in his own house in St. Johnston, on the 5th August, 1600, for treason against the king,* of intention to have murdered him, having invited him to his own house. Their dead bodies were carried to Edinburgh, and their heads put upon the most eminent places of justice in that town. The story is extant in divers languages, but, for the truth of the narration, it is not fit to be dived into here: *Nam rimanda non sunt arcana imperii.* William was banished to France, and there died; and Patrick was kept many years in the Tower of London, where, by his own industry, he attained to a great knowledge in physic; but, because he took no fees for it, he came never to great riches.

The earldom was divided by the king among the three who had been most active at their slaughter, viz., John Ramsay the page, whom the king made Viscount of Haddington; Sir Thomas Areskine, created Earl of Kelly; and Sir Hugh Herries. Haddington was afterwards made Earl of Holderness, and died in great favour with the king; but all the lands that he got, and what he conquest himself, are disponed by his successors. In like manner, the barony of Cousland, given to the said Sir Hugh Herries, remained but very few years with him, being evicted by law from his relict. And of the Earl of Kelly's, only the barony of Kelly and Pittenweem conquest

---

1583. Having conspired a second time to seize the person of the young king, he was apprehended and arraigned for high treason. He was found guilty, and condemned on the 4th May, 1584, and executed on the same day. By his wife, second daughter of Henry, Lord Methven, he had five sons and seven daughters.

* The reality of the Gowrie conspiracy was long doubted by the Presbyterian party, who conceived that the Earl of Gowrie and his brother fell victims to the unrighteous policy which had sacrificed their father. Modern historians, including Mr. Tytler, are, however, entirely of opinion that the conspiracy was a reality, and that the king's life was, according to his relation of the event, seriously imperilled.

by himself remain undisposed. For the lordship of Dirleton was sold by himself twenty years ago to James Maxwell, one of the bedchamber: and this present earl having been at the battle of Worcester in England, and taken prisoner, is said to have escaped, and come privately to Scotland in a beggar's habit.*

4. Thomas, master of Glammis, treasurer. He was brother to the Lord Glammis, chancellor, who was shot in Stirling out of a window, riding through the streets.†

He was one of them who attended the king in his minority in the castle of Stirling. It was he that, long before he came to that place, at the Raid of Stirling, *anno* 1585, when King James was pressing to go out at the castle-gate to the lords who came to take him, put his foot to the gate, and held the king in; who, then weeping for anger, got that answer from the master, *'tis better bairns weep as bearded men.* Yet for all that, the king honoured him with that place. ‡

He was a bold man, and stout; and because that he was informed that the Earl of Crawfurd was the author of his brother's death, he came with some of his friends to the house of Cairny, in Fife, there to have killed the said earl, having before agreed with his chamber-boy to betray him to them; but there being one of the master's company in the close, attending at the time when the servant should give a sign for their coming, the servant, upon remorse, revealed the plot to my lord, and having shown him the place where the man stood in the close, he with a single bullet killed him dead; whereupon the master and his company behoved to retire.

He conquest the barony of Auldbar, and other lands, but had no succession; so that his estate fell to the Lord Kinghorn's brother James, and is since acquired by his brother the Earl of Kinghorn.

5. Walter Stewart, commendator of Blantyre, brother to the laird of Minto, treasurer in King James VI.'s time. When he was

---

* After the execution of the first Earl of Gowrie, the Earl of Montrose was preferred to the post of treasurer. He held the office about a year; he subsequently became Lord High Chancellor (see *supra*).

† See *supra*.

‡ Sir Thomas Lyon was one of the chief conspirators at the Raid of Ruthven. In October 1585 he succeeded in driving the favourite Arran from the king's presence, when he obtained restoration of his estates which had been forfeited, and was constituted Lord High Treasurer for life. He demitted the treasurership on being appointed in 1596 one of the Octavians. He died 18th February, 1608.

riding up the street of Edinburgh, he fell and broke his leg, and a courtier said, merrily, that it was no marvel the horse could not bear him, seeing he had so many offices ingrossed in his person; for by that place he was a lord of council, session, and exchequer. He conquest the baronies of Blantyre, Cardonald, and Calderhall.*

His eldest son, James, married Lady Dorothy Hastings, daughter to the Earl of Huntington. When he went up to England with King James he was in great favour with his majesty, being a gallant youth of great hopes; but a discord falling out betwixt him and the young Lord Wharton, they went out to single combat, each against the other, a mile from London, and, at the first thrust, each of them killed the other, and fell dead in one another's arms upon the place.

The second son, William, Lord Blantyre, sold Calderhall to Harie Elphinston: and I believe little or nothing is left of the lands unwadset or undisposed at this day.

6. Alexander, Lord Elphinston, was treasurer some years before the king's going to England.† His family had its first rise in King James IV.'s time, by marrying Elizabeth Barlie, an Englishwoman, one of the queen's maids: for with her the king gave him the lordship of Kildrimmie.

He lived till he attained a great age; but the king moved him to quit the place to Sir George Home, a courtier.

His son, the master of Elphinston, having no heirs male, the lordship fell to another brother's son, who has got it with so great a burden of debt that it is suspected ‡ that it shall end in his person.

* Walter Stewart was son of Sir John Stewart, of Minto; he was born about the year 1568, and was, along with James VI., educated under Buchannan. He was in 1595, appointed one of the Octavians, and in the following year Lord High Treasurer. He held the office for three years. In 1606 he was raised to the peerage by the title of Lord Blantyre. He died in March, 1617, and was succeeded by James his eldest son, who was killed in a duel by Sir George Wharton, on the 8th November, 1609.—(Crawfurd's Officers of State).

† On the removal of Walter Stewart from the Treasurership, the office was bestowed on Gilbert, Earl of Cassilis, who resigned it after a short period. He was succeeded by Alexander, Lord Elphinston, who demitted the office after a year. He died July, 1648, at an advanced age.

‡ Our author's surmise as to the speedy downfall of the House of Elphinstone has not been realized. John, 13th Baron Elphinstone, was, for his distinguished services as Governor of Bombay, raised to the British peerage 21st May, 1859. He died 19th July, 1860, when he was succeeded by his cousin, the present peer.

In his time there was a process intented against him by the Earl of Mar for the lordship of Kildrimmie, as a part of that earldom, and the same was evicted; at least, by transaction for great sums of money, was disponed again to him.

7. Sir George Home * was in great credit with King James after his going to England, and by him was created first Lord of Berwick, then Earl of Dunbar. He got all these offices erected in his person, and was made treasurer, comptroller, and collector, and was sent many times to Scotland, as the king's commissioner, to execute justice on the borders, which he did with great rigour: but, by the hatred of some of the courtiers there, he was not suffered long to enjoy that extraordinary favour; for with some tablets of sugar, given him for expelling the cold by Secretary Cecil, he was poisoned: which was well known by the death of Martin Sougar, a doctor, who, by laying his finger on his heart, and touching it with his tongue, died within a few days thereafter; and by the relation of his servant of his chamber, Sir James Baillie, who saw him get the tablets from the said secretary, and who having eaten a small parcel of them himself, struck all out in blisters; but by strength of body he escaped death.

His estate, being very great, fell to his two daughters. The one married the Lord Walden, an Englishman; the other the laird of Cowdenknowes. The Lord Walden disponed all his part thereof, viz., the lordship of Berwick, to Sir James Douglas, the Earl of Angus's brother, after he had caused pull down the great edifice of the castle of Berwick, that he had built there, and transported the

---

* Sir George Home was third son of Alexander Home, of Manderston, Berwickshire. In early life he was introduced at court, and being a favourite of the king, he soon attained emoluments and honours. He was appointed Treasurer on the 5th September, 1601. When James succeeded to the English throne, Home followed him to London. He became Chancellor of the English Exchequer, and was created Baron Home. He was subsequently created Earl of Dunbar, in the peerage of Scotland. He zealously aided the king in his designs to overthrow Presbyterianism; and his manners being conciliatory, he endeavoured to reconcile the Presbyterian clergy to the prelatic system. An able administrator, he was frequently employed on special services. He died at Whitehall, on the 29th January, 1611. The story of his death, as related in the text, is pure fiction —one of those calumnies which our author was unhappily too prone to indulge. In the parish church of Dunbar, the Earl of Dunbar is commemorated by an elegantly sculptured marble monument of massive proportions.

whole marble other and hewn work thereof to London. The other son-in-law, Cowdenknowes, despatched also his part, and sold the same to Thomas, Earl of Haddington. Yet did his son, procreated on the said Earl of Dunbar's daughter, by law attain to the earldom of Home, which was worth £5,000 *sterl. per annum.* But, in the space of five years, it is brought to such a pass, that little or nothing is left thereof, scarce so much as to sustain him and his family.

8. Sir Robert Ker,* a brother of the house of Fernihirst, became minion to the king about the year 1608, and by him was raised to great honours, and made first Lord Rochester, and then Earl of Somerset and Knight of the Garter. By the death of the foresaid Earl of Dunbar he got established in his person the places of treasury, comptrollery, and collectory, which he exercised never by himself, but by his depute, Sir Gideon Murray, his near kinsman, who shall be spoken hereafter.

He married the Countess of Essex, being divorced from her husband for his inability. But that lady, having a great spleen at his friend, Sir Thomas Overbury, who dissuaded him from that marriage, and told him it would never thrive, she thereupon counselled her husband to cause the king send Sir Thomas ambassador to Persia or Turkey, for disobeying of which command he was committed prisoner to the Tower, and there, by the said lady's moyen, he was poisoned; and she thereafter and her husband were indicted and convicted of murder, and condemned for that fact; but, by the favour of court, their lives were preserved.

He had no heirs male, but married his only daughter to the Earl of Bedford, and gave him so great a portion with her, that he had very small means to live upon himself before his death; and the burdens of the lands in Scotland, which he had acquired off the house of Fernihirst, being taken on and paid by his brother-in-law, the Lord Balmerino, were so great, that it is likely little or nothing thereof will accresce to the said lady or her husband, whereupon they have at present a Process depending before the judges in Scotland.

* On the death of the Earl of Dunbar, the treasurership was put into commission. It was bestowed on Sir Robert Ker, in 1613, who was the same year created Viscount Rochester. In 1614 he was appointed Lord Chamberlain, and advanced to the earldom of Somerset. The leading events in the subsequent career of this unprincipled courtier are by our author correctly related. He died at London, in July, 1645.—Crawfurd's "Officers of State."

9. John, Earl of Mar,* got all the offices of treasury, comptrollery, and collectory, after the death of Sir Gideon Murray, which he discharged many years. Yet was his estate nothing bettered thereby; for albeit he conquest the lordship of Carnwath, belonging to the Lord Somerville, to the eldest son procreated of the Duke of Lennox's sister, and got him the earldom of Buchan by marrying the heritrix thereof, yet for all that it evanished, and melted like snow off a dyke; Carnwath being sold to Sir Robert Dalziel, and the rest of the lands being all apprised by his cautioners, and they in possession of the same.

His chief delight was in hunting, and he procured by acts of parliament that none should hunt within divers miles of the king's house. Yet often that which is most pleasant to a man is his overthrow; for, walking in his own hall, a dog cast him off his feet and lamed his leg, of which he died; and at his burial, a hare having run through the company, his special chamberlain, Alexander Stirling, fell off his horse and broke his neck.

He sold many lands in his own time, as the lordship of Brechin and Navarre; the barony of Walstoun to Robert Baillie, the barony of Coldinghoof to James Rae, the whole spiritualities and teinds of the abbacies of Dryburgh, Cambuskenneth, and Inchmaholm.

His eldest son being put off the session, as being a nobleman, and having returned home, became blind, as he is at this day; and the burdens of the estate are yet thought to be great enough, and that John Knox's prophecy is like to take effect, who said that House could not long subsist, being so sacrilegious.†

---

* John, seventh Earl of Mar, son of the Regent Mar, was born in 1558. He was, along with James VI., educated at Stirling under Buchanan. He joined in the Raid of Ruthven, and was forfeited, but afterwards received the royal pardon. He was entrusted with the charge of Prince Henry, accompanied James VI. to London, and was sworn of the English Privy Council, and installed a Knight of the Garter. He was appointed Treasurer of Scotland on the fall of Somerset in December, 1615; he resigned office in 1630. Lord Mar died at Stirling on the 14th December, 1634.

† The Regent Mar completed the destruction of Cambuskenneth Abbey, and with the materials erected an elegant private mansion in a conspicuous position on Stirling Rock. John Knox, it is related, remonstrated with him on the impropriety of demolishing a religious house to suit his private ends, but without changing the regent's purpose. To indicate his contempt of ecclesiastical interference, he caused these inscriptions to be engraved over the chief entrances of his mansion :—

10. William, Earl of Morton,* treasurer, was son of the laird of Lochleven, who in his youth, with his sister's son, Lord Oliphant, fled out of the country, for cutting off four loads of spears carried from St. Johnston to Stirling, thinking they had been my Lord Hamilton's, with whom he had deadly feud, for the slaughter of the good regent, James, Earl of Murray, when indeed they belonged to his majesty; for which reason he left the kingdom, but upon his travels he perished in the sea.

So William, Earl of Morton, succeeded to his grandfather; but disponed the most part of the lands in his time, to wit, the lordship of Morton, the baronies of Drochils, Linton, and Carnebothell the lordship of Eskdale-muir, and Kirknewton, the lordship and regality of Dalkeith, to the value of £100,000 *Scots* of yearly rent.

He continued short time in the place, and quitted the same wholly to the Earl of Traquair, after he had got a great sum of money from the king for quitting of Dalkeith.

Thereafter he got Orkney and the small customs, to which country he went, and there died; and nothing of that vast estate is now left except Aberdour and Lochleven, upon which there are as great burdens as will exhaust them.

He himself and his son both begot adulterous children; at least the father was known to have disregarded his lady, and to have had conversation with others in her time; and his son begot a child on a servant-maid when his wife was in childbed. In a short time after his father's death he died also.

What they have in Orkney by the late king's gift cannot now subsist in law, if it be challenged, as being land gotten unlawfully

---

"I pray al lvkaris on this lvging,
Vith gentil e to gif thair jvging."

"The moir I stand on opin hitht,
My faults mair svbiect are to sitht."

"Esspy, speik furth, and spair notcht,
Considder veil I cair notht."

* William, Earl of Morton, was born in 1587. He was constituted Treasurer in April, 1630, and held the office five years. A stanch adherent of Charles I., he sold his estate of Dalkeith to procure money for that monarch. On the outbreak of the Civil War he retired to his estate in Orkney. He died on the 7th August, 1648, in his sixty-first year.

by an advice of lawyers, making the king acknowledge the receipt of great sums from a man who never had any to give him.

11. Sir John Stewart of Traquair, knight, thereafter created Earl of Traquair, was first brought in by the Earl of Morton to be treasurer-depute to him, but within a few years he displaced the principal,* and got the full possession of the treasury to himself; which place he managed so nimbly that he conquest many lands in the space that he enjoyed the same,† to wit, the baronies of Drochils, Linton Horseburgh, Henderland, Dryhope, and many others. He was, as Lucian said, *impatiens consortis*. For, finding himself opposed in judicatories by the kirkmen, called bishops, he rested not till he got them undermined and by act of parliament expelled the kingdom. And their own insolence, pride, and avarice gave him good ground to do so; for they could not be content with their bishopricks, but urged also to have all the rest of the kirk-livings, as abbacies, priories, &c., which exasperated the whole kingdom against them.

In these times the said Lord Traquair, after subscribing the Covenant, went up to court, and there in public council declared against the public resolutions of the kingdom of Scotland; which was the first ground that moved the English to consent to levy an army against this nation; with which army the king himself came down to the Border. But matters being then pacified, the said Earl of Traquair was made the king's commissioner to the parliament; but after that was declared incapable of government, and an in-

* The Earl of Traquair was appointed Treasurer in 1635. When Charles I. thrust the Liturgy on the Scottish Church in 1637, he took a prominent part in executing the king's command. He afterwards subscribed the Covenant, and became High Commissioner to the General Assembly of 1639, which ratified the proceedings of the famous Assembly of the former year, abolishing episcopacy and rescinding the Articles of Perth. In 1641 he was impeached before the Scottish Parliament as "an incendiary"; he was rescued from a capital sentence by receiving the royal pardon, but was deprived of the Treasurership. In 1648 he raised a troop of horse in connexion with "the Engagement." Taken prisoner at the battle of Preston, he was warded in Warwick Castle, where he remained a prisoner four years. He died suddenly on the 27th March, 1659. In a note to Goodal's edition of this work, it is related that he died in extreme poverty. This writer adds, "At his burial he had no mortcloth but a black apron; nor towels, but dogs' leishes belonging to some gentlemen that were present; and the grave being two feet shorter than his body, the assistants behoved to stay till the same was enlarged and he buried."·

† He was Treasurer from 1636 till 1641.

cendiary, by act of parliament, and behoved to retire to England; where being with the king, and having dealt for the releasing the Earl of Lothian, then prisoner there (after his return from France, and seeking supply to Scotland from the said kingdom), he obtained such favour and respect of the said earl, that by his means he was brought in again to the parliament, wherein the engagement against England was concluded; with the which army he went himself, and was taken prisoner at Preston, where he has been detained since.

One George Nicol, a writer, gave in a paper to the king against him, when he was in his grandeur, showing that many of the king's rents were misguided; but he got no other thanks nor reward from his majesty, but he remitted him to the censure of the council, who decerned him to be scourged, a paper put on his head, and to stand at the cross of Edinburgh a forenoon; which made the poor young man fly the country, and terrified all other persons from informing his majesty of any thing that was done to his prejudice in this kingdom.

He also procured from his majesty a remission to one Thomas Mackie, sheriff-clerk of Wigton, who was found guilty by the sentence of the lords of session of a notable falsehood, viz., to have filled up, in a small piece of paper cut out of the first leaf of a Bible, whereon the Lord Herries's name was written, before that word *Herries* (which was done for knowing the book to be his) a discharge of 6,000 merks, which a gentleman in the country was owing to the said Lord Herries, and insert four dead witnesses therein, that it might never be gotten improven. For this, it was said, he got 5,000 merks, whether of composition to the king, or for his own use, is best known to himself. Which truly has done great prejudice to the kingdom, and opened a door to many, who, in imitation thereof, have since counterfeited writs, and have been convicted and hanged for so doing.

Another great prejudice he did to the nation: for when some Dutchmen, as assignies to the Earls of Panmure and Stirling, had got a liberty of trading in Guinea for Scotland, as the English had before, and had brought a ship to Leith with the commodities of the said land, and much gold in dust to be coined there, the said Treasurer did so cross the merchant, Mr. Hieronymus Leffell, by delays and rigorous exaction of dues never before heard of, and by the means of a servant of the master-coiner's, cousin-german to his lady, who run away with a pockful of the said gold, that the poor man broke his heart, and died in Edinburgh in a few days, and that trade was renounced for ever after, to the no small discredit of the Scots nation in Germany; of which nation all the undertakers were natives.

He has lived a prisoner since that time, and is said now to have turned a preacher. His only son, the Lord Linton, within these few years, married the Lady Seton, an excommunicate Papist.

The father has been much slandered for his too much familiarity with the ladies of Monteith and Cardross, the verity whereof none knows but God and himself. And if they be true, it is likely that his family will not be of long subsistence, albeit he has done the utmost of his endeavours for establishing the same to posterity: for it is no marvel he grew rich, seeing he never made compt of his intromissions with the king's rents, many years before his departure.

12. John, Earl of Crawfurd,* brother-in-law to the Duke of Hamilton, after the battle of Longmeston-muir, where the king's nephew, Prince Rupert, was defeated, was, by the parliament, appointed Treasurer for the king, and kept the place but three or four years; and it may be justly said of him as the Romans said of Bibulus:—

"Et Bibulo memini consule nil fieri."

For in his time he neither did good to the king, himself, nor his friends; but having 100,000 merks of his own, he has spent the same, and hurt the rest of his lands in a high measure.

He had a liberty, by patent under the great seal, ratified in parliament, for changing the whole ward-lands into feu, which might have been of great benefit to the king and to himself also, if he had put the same in practice. But albeit many urged to have got their lands changed, yet did he never suffer any at all to pass but one charter of his own.

His dependence and following of the house of Hamilton has much harmed him, and by their council was he moved to condescend to that engagement; since which time he has been in great

---

* John, eleventh Lord Lindsay, and fourteenth Earl of Crawfurd, was constituted Treasurer in 1641. He joined the "Engagement" of 1648, and in the following year was deprived of his Treasurership by the Estates. At the coronation of Charles II., at Scone, in 1650, he carried the sceptre. After the Restoration he was replaced in the Treasurership, which he resigned in favour of the Earl of Rothes, his son-in-law, in 1664. He died in 1676.

hatred by the kingdom, and debarred from all public trust; till, by consent of the Church, and authority of the General Assembly, all malignants were brought in to expel the enemy; at which time his majesty left him to raise forces in the north, with some other of the nobility; where, with his associates, he was apprehended at Eliott, in August, or September, 1651, and was sent prisoner to London, where he was incarcerate in the Tower, and there detained till the return of King Charles II.

Treasurer-Deputes.

1. Sir Robert Melville, of Murdocairnie, was Treasurer-depute in King James VI.'s time,* and therein did very good service, which appears by the success of his posterity: for albeit his only son, Sir Robert Melville, had never children, yet his conquests are as yet entire to the heirs of tailzie. Only this wrong was done by his son, Robert Lord Melville, that he gave the title and best part of his lands to the house of Raith, of which house he himself was descended, and made them Lords Melville, when indeed the laird of Halhill was righteous heir.† Yet the barony of Burntisland of old pertained to the abbot of Dunfermline, who was chief instrument in the governor's time, to take the head off the said laird of Raith for having written a letter ‡ to an Englishman; and yet so ruled Divine Providence, that, by the favour of King James VI., he got the heritable right of

* Sir Robert Melville was second son of the laird of Raith. Though a convert to the Reformed doctrines, he zealously upheld the cause of Queen Mary, and was on her behalf often sent as ambassador to the English Court. He was appointed Treasurer-depute and knighted in 1582. In December, 1586, he was sent to England by James VI., along with the Master of Gray, to plead with Queen Elizabeth for his mother's life. When, in 1589, James sailed for Norway to bring home his queen, he appointed Melville Vice-Chancellor of the kingdom. In 1594 he was admitted an extraordinary Lord of Session. He resigned his depute-treasurership in 1596, on the appointment of the Octavians. He was created Lord Melville of Monimail on the 30th April, 1616. He died in 1621, at the advanced age of ninety-four.

† Robert, second Lord Melville, was twice married, but dying without issue, he was succeeded by his cousin, son of John Melville of Raith, his father's eldest brother. Our author complains that the honours were not allowed to descend in the line of conquest, in which case Sir James Melville, of Halhill, the first Lord Melville's younger brother, would have been heir. Sir John Scot married, as his second wife, Margaret Melville, daughter of the Laird of Halhill.

‡ Sir John Melville, of Raith, father of Sir Robert, afterwards Lord Melville,

that barony by their extirpation. Nevertheless, in these unhappy times, the same is fallen into the hands of the English, and, except they favour him, the said laird of Halhill will lose of yearly rent four hundred bolls of bear, with the castle and gardens lying above the town.

2. Sir John Arnot, of *Bersick*,* Provost of Edinburgh, Treasurer-depute under the Earl of Dunbar, conquest a good estate, viz., 200,000 merks, upon a comprising of Orkney and Zetland, of which sum his majesty made payment to him after the forfeiture of the said earl, to the end he might come to the possession of the said earldom of Orkney. He conquest also the baronies of Cockburnspath, and lands of Woodmill in Fife. To his eldest son, John, he gave the lands, and a great stock of money to his son James, a merchant, who, within a few years after his decease, by his cautionry for James Dalziel, made bankrupt of all, and fled the country.† His grandson John, son to the said John Arnot of Cockburnspath, sold the barony to Mr. James Nicolson, advocate: so that of all that estate and conquest nothing now remains but seven or eight chalders of victual, possessed by John Arnot his grandson.

3. Sir Gideon Murray, brother to the laird of Black-barony, was Treasurer-depute under the Earl of Somerset, but full Treasurer in effect. In his younger age he studied theology; but having unhappily killed a man called Aitchison, was for that slaughter imprisoned in the castle of Edinburgh, and, being a well-favoured youth, got favour from Captain James Stewart's lady, who then ruled all, and by her means was released, and got a remission. After that he was employed by the laird of Buccleuch to manage his estate, when he went

---

was in 1550, at the instance of Archbishop Hamilton, and his relative, George Duric, Abbot of Dunfermline, charged with conducting a treasonable correspondence in England, and after a mock trial was condemned and executed. He was a zealous promoter of the Reformation.

* A scion of the ancient house of Arnot of that ilk, Sir John Arnot, of Berswick, Orkney, was in 1587 chosen Lord Provost of Edinburgh for four years. In 1604 he was appointed Treasurer-depute of Scotland. Beside extensive possessions in Orkney, he acquired lands in the counties of Fife, Berwick, and Midlothian (Hugo Arnot's "MS. Genealogy of the Arnots, in the Lyon Office").

† John Dalziel, merchant in Edinburgh, married a daughter of Sir John Arnot of Berswick. Consequent on his bankruptcy his brothers-in-law, William Arnot of Cockburnspath, and James Arnot of Granton, were obliged to sell their estates (Hugo Arnot's MS.).

to his travels in Italy; where he bettered his own estate in a good measure, and carried the laird's standard, with five hundred of the name of Scot, against my Lord Maxwell, where the said Lord Maxwell was killed: the which Lord Maxwell had invaded the laird of Johnstone, who was sister's son to the laird of Buccleuch, who had with him a great army.

Thereafter he lived a private man till the year 1613, or thereby, at which time he was advanced to be treasurer by his cousin the Earl of Somerset, which place he discharged notably, and not only repaired all the king's decayed houses, viz. Holyrood House, the castle of Edinburgh, Linlithgow, Stirling, Dunfermline, Falkland, and Dunbarton, but added to them all new great edifices, and had so much money in the king's coffers at King James VI.'s coming to Scotland in 1617, that therewith he defrayed the king's whole charges, and those of his court, during his abode in Scotland; whereby he was so well loved and respected of his majesty, that, when he went thereafter to the court of England, there being none in the bedchamber but the king, the said Sir Gideon and myself, Sir Gideon by chance letting his chevron fall to the ground, the king, although being both stiff and old, stooped down and gave him his glove, saying, "My predecessor, Queen Elizabeth, thought she did a favour to any man who was speaking with her when she let her glove fall, that he might take it up and give it her again; but, sir, you may say a king lifted up your glove." Yet, for all that, within few years thereafter, all these services were forgot, and his majesty was induced to believe calumnies given in, in a paper, by Sir James Stewart, son to Captain James, who was afterwards styled Ochiltree; and being sent for to court, was challenged of sundry misdemeanours, and sent home as a prisoner, and a day appointed for his trial by such judges as the king should appoint: whereat he took such grief and sorrow of heart, that he took bed, and abstained absolutely from meat for many days, imagining that he had no money either to get meat or drink to himself, and that way died, after a fortnight's sickness, of abstinence. Yet his family stands, and his son, Sir Patrick, was made a lord of parliament by King Charles; but, by alliance of his son with the house of Traquair, he quitted the right side, and took him to the malignants, and shortly thereafter died. How the estate will thrive will be known in the third generation.*

* Sir Gideon Murray was some time chamberlain to his nephew, Sir Walter Scott, of Buccleuch. In the parliament which met at Edinburgh, in October,

4. Sir Archibald Napier of Merchiston was the son of that learned Merchiston who wrote a Logarithmy, and a Commentary upon the Revelation. He was Treasurer-depute under the Earl of Mar, but augmented his estate noways in that time.

He obtained the favour of his majesty, after long service, of being a gentleman of the privy-chamber, but was, by the power of the Earl of Traquair, thrust out of that place, and behoved to accept a certain sum of money of composition for his kindness of the same. He was created a lord of parliament at that time; but thereafter both he and his eldest son, the master, who was sister's son to Montrose, having adhered to his party, was forced to fly: the father fled to the Highlands, where he died; and the son fled out of the country, who, being robbed of all his money in his way towards Paris, still lives there, and his lands are forfeited.*

SECRETARIES.

1. Sir William Maitland of Lethington, Secretary,† albeit a man of good parts and learning, yet was he never fast nor solid in his ways; for sometimes was he for the congregation, and sometimes

---

1612, he was member for Selkirkshire. Sir Robert Ker, on being appointed Treasurer in 1613, nominated him Treasurer-depute. In November of the same year he was admitted a Lord of Session. He died on the 28th June, 1621. By his wife, Margaret Pentland, he had two sons and a daughter, Agnes, who married Sir William Scott, of Harden, eldest son of "The Flower of Yarrow." Sir Patrick, his elder son, was created a Baronet of Nova Scotia in 1628, and raised to the peerage as Lord Elibank in 1643 (Anderson's "Scottish Nation").

* Sir Archibald Napier, as gentleman of the Privy Chamber, accompanied James VI. to London in 1603. He was constituted Treasurer-depute 21st October, 1622, and a Lord of Session in the following year. In March, 1627, he was created a Baronet of Nova Scotia, and was raised to the peerage as Baron Napier, of Merchiston, in May, 1627. On the outbreak of the Civil War he actively supported the cause of Charles I., and by the ruling party was subjected to imprisonment and heavy penalties. Liberated by his son, the master of Napier, after the battle of Kilsyth, he joined the Marquis of Montrose, and after the defeat at Philiphaugh, escaped with him into Athol. He there died in November, 1645. His son Archibald, second Lord Napier, died in Holland, in 1660.

† Our author's estimate of Secretary Maitland is entirely borne out by the testimony of contemporary writers. Totally destitute of principle, Maitland was foremost among the many unstable statesmen of his period. An early promoter of the Reformation, he resisted the designs of the Regent, Mary of Guise, to arrest its progress, and presided in the Parliament of 1560, which abolished Papal worship.

for the queen. The Earl of Murray, regent, for all that took him to England, and almost against his will; thinking it unsafe to leave him behind him, being a factious man. And at that time was a letter of his intercepted, written to the queen, wherein he said "he might prove like the mouse that rid the lion of her snares;" and the time that Murray and he were in York, he nightly met with the Queen of Scotland's ambassador. He was the firebrand of all the conjurations betwixt the Scots queen and the Lord Norfolk against Queen Elizabeth. And for that the Earl of Murray, by the accusation of one Crawford against him, as being art and part of the king's murder, sent him prisoner; and being kept in a house near the castle by a number of horsemen, the laird of Grange, captain of the castle, by counterfeiting the regent's warrant, got him delivered to him by Alexander Home, captain of the said troop; in which castle he was kept till the day on which he was summoned to answer; at which day he got all the Hamiltons and the queen's party to assist him, so that the regent behoved to delay the diet till another time. A little after that, the regent being killed, he was again admitted to the council, and nothing was done in the queen's faction without his advice, albeit he was lying of the gout; so that his chamber was called the school, and these his scholars.

When the ministers solicited him for leave to preach, he gave himself to the devil, if, after that day, he should regard what became of them, and bade them bark and blow as they listed.*

His estate stood not long after his own death, but was taken from

---

In 1562, to gratify Queen Mary, he promoted an impeachment against John Knox, which might have cost the Reformer his life. In 1566 he joined the conspiracy against Rizzio, and in the following year aided Bothwell in the murder of Darnley. He now joined the confederacy against Bothwell, and concurring in the Queen's dethronement, was present in July, 1567, at the coronation of the infant James. He aided the Queen's escape from Lochleven, and thereafter took part against her at Langside. One of the commissioners who accused her at York, he privately conspired with the Duke of Norfolk to effect her restoration to the throne. Attainted by Parliament in May, 1571, he was sheltered, by Kirkaldy of Grange, in Edinburgh Castle, but on its surrender in May, 1573, he was taken prisoner by the Regent Morton. He died in prison, on the 9th June, 1573. According to Calderwood, it was reported that he took poison.

* Our author makes this statement on the authority of Calderwood, whom, however, he misquotes, since the words attributed to the Secretary were not expressed in answer to any address or solicitation presented to him, but after a sermon on

his son by Sir John Maitland, chancellor, without sums of money; and his son James behoved to quit Scotland, being a papist, and died at Brussels, having neither lands nor money, but what he begged of the Infanta there. This was foretold by Knox in his History, printed 1644,* fol. 375, where he says, that, after a preaching which he had on Haggai, the said William Maitland said in mockage, "We may now forget ourselves, and bear the barrow to build the house of God." "God be merciful to the speaker," says Knox; "for we fear yet that he shall have experience that the building of his own house, the house of God being despised, shall not be so prosperous." And fol. 376, speaking of Lethington, he says "that he was fully assured, as he was assured that God lives, that some that heard this his defection against the truth and servants of God, should see a part of God's judgments poured forth upon the realm, and principally upon him that fastest cleaves to the favour of the court." †

2. Mr. John Lindsay, parson of Menmuir, a brother of the House of Edzel, was secretary to King James VI. in his majority, and one of the Octavians, who, for their council and strict dealing with the people, were so hateful, that the commonality of the town of Edinburgh, on the 17th day of December, 1597, rose in arms, when they were sitting in the session-house, to have killed him and the rest in the king's majesty's presence; but by his majesty's presence they were saved at that time, and the tumult pacified.

He was of good learning, but of a sickly body, and died in his middle age. ‡

---

hypocrisy, preached by Mr. Craig, John Knox's colleague (Calderwood's "History of the Kirk of Scotland." Edinburgh, 1871, 8vo., vol. ii. p. 249).

* The edition of Knox's History, published at London in 1644, and reprinted at Edinburgh in the same year, was edited by David Buchanan. It is altogether worthless, many passages being omitted, and others interpolated, including those quoted by our author.

† After Maitland, of Lethington, Robert Pitcairn, commendator of Dunfermline, was secretary from 1572 till 1583. Sir John Maitland, of Thirlestane, was secretary in 1584, and both chancellor and secretary in 1587. Sir Richard Cockburn, of Clerkington, was secretary in 1591; he demitted in 1595.

‡ John Lindsay, styled "Parson of Menmuir," from his holding the teinds of that parish, was second son of Sir David Lindsay, of Edzell, ninth Earl of Crawford; he was born in 1552. He studied law, and in 1581 was appointed a Lord of Session, when he assumed the judicial title of Lord Menmuir. In January, 1595, he was appointed one of the Octavians, or eight commissioners of exche-

His conquests were not thought very lawful ; for having married the wife of umquhil Mr. David Borthwick, the king's advocate, and that way got the sight of the writs, he conquest the lands of Balcarras from David's son, being a spendthrift. His haill conquest was about threescore ten chalders of victual.

His son Sir David was made a lord of parliament,* and his grandson Alexander, now Lord Balcarras, has been colonel of a regiment of horse in the late troubles ; but never did any service to the country, but fled at six battles, when Montrose overrun the land *in annis* 1643, 1644, and 1645 ; and, at King Charles II.'s command, his troops being sent to Inverkeithing were totally defeated by the English ; but himself then was employed as the king's commissioner to the General Assembly at Dundee, where he was sitting the time of the defeat *in anno* 1651. From thence he fled to the north, where he has hitherto remained: but what estate he shall leave to his posterity is yet unknown ; for *finis coronat opus*.

3. Mr. James Elphinston, brother to the Lord Elphinston,† was

quer. In May, 1596, he was nominated Secretary of State of life, but he resigned the office at the close of the following year. He died on the 3rd September, 1598, in his 47th year. Lord Menmuir was an able lawyer, a ripe scholar, and an accomplished statesman. His collection of letters and state papers are preserved in the Advocates Library (Lord Lindsay's " Lives of the Lindsays ").

* Sir David Lindsay (knighted in 1612) was devoted to literary and scientific studies, which he prosecuted at Balcarres, his family seat. In June, 1633, he was created Lord Lindsay, of Balcarres. He died in March, 1641. His eldest son, Alexander, second Lord Balcarres, was on the side of the Covenanters, present at the battles of Alford and Kilsyth. He joined the "engagement" of 1648, and afterwards vigorously supported the cause of Charles II. In 1651 he was created Earl of Balcarres, and nominated hereditary governor of Edinburgh Castle. He upheld the royal cause against Cromwell, but was defeated, and had his estates sequestrated. He afterwards proceeded to France, and attended Charles II. as Secretary of State. He died at Breda on the 30th August, 1659. The poet Cowley composed his elegy. (" Lives of the Lindsays ").

† Sir James Elphinstone, of Innernochtie, was third son of Robert, third Lord Elphinstone. He was appointed a Lord of Session in 1586, and one of the Octavians, or Commissioners of Exchequer, in 1595. In 1596 he became Secretary of State, and in 1604 was raised to the peerage by the title of Lord Balmerino. In 1599 he drew up a letter to the Pope, Clement VIII., entreating the dignity of Cardinal for his kinsman, Chisholme, Bishop of Vaison, and placing the document among other papers, surreptitiously procured to it the king's signature. The deceit was discovered in 1608, when Balmerino confessed his guilt. The proceedings subsequent to his confession are circumstantially related in the text. He died in his house at Balmerino in 1612.

one of the Octavians, and Secretary after the death of the said Mr. John Lindsay, a man of a notable spirit and great gifts, as he gave proof at his being in England as one of the commissioners for the treaty of union *in anno* 1605.

He was in such favour with King James, that he craved the reversion of Secretary Cecil's place, at the king's coming to the crown of England, which was the beginning of his overthrow; for the said Secretary Cecil wrought so, that having procured a letter which had come from King James, wherein he promised all kindness to the Roman see and pope, if his holiness would assist him to attain to the crown of England; this letter the said Secretary Cecil showed in the king's presence in the council of England; whereupon King James, fearing to displease the English nation, behoved to disclaim the penning of this letter, and lay the blame thereof on his secretary whom, a little before that, he had made Lord Balmerino; to whom he wrote to come to court; where being come, for exoneration of the king, he behoved to take on him the guilt of writing that letter. And therefore was he sent back to Scotland with the Earl of Dunbar as a prisoner, first to Edinburgh, with the people of which place he was little favoured, because he had acquired many lands about the town, as Restalrig, Barnetoun, and mills of Leith; so that James Henderson, the bailie, forced him to light off his horse at the foot of Leithwynd, albeit he had the rose in his leg and was very unable to walk, till he came to the prison-house. Some days thereafter he was accused of treason, and then sent prisoner to Falkland, and at last carried to St. Andrews, and there sentenced to want the head, but no time prefixed when.

Thereafter he got liberty to go to his own house of Balmerino, where, being a widower, he got an amatorious potion of cantharides from a maid in his house called Young (thereafter wife to Doctor Honeyman) of which he died.

He got the two abbacies of Balmerino and Cowpar erected into two temporal lordships by his majesty. His conquests were not thought good, neither of Balumbie nor Restalrig; for of the first he got the evidents from Balwearie, and having taken assignations to the debts, comprised the land, and got the heritor's gift of escheat and liferent, by that means came into possession. Yet his son, John, Lord Balmerino, moved in conscience, gave to James Lovall, son to Cunnoquhie, 10,000 merks. And, for Restalrig, it was vulgarly said, that, at the laird's death, he was owing him a great sum of money; to be freed of the payment whereof he found means to get the said laird forfeited, as being an assistant in Gowrie's conspiracy; which was proven by one Sprott, a notary; and Sprott being condemned for other falsehoods, confessed that, with other things, before he was cast over the gallows; but *vox populi* said he had assurance that the Earl of Dunbar should have holden out a napkin to have saved him. But after his hanging, Restalrig's body was raised up and forfeited, and the gift of forfeiture given to the said Balmerino, whereby he was freed from payment of the said sum. The public report was, that after his decease he caused his body to be secretly in the night time thrown in the river Tay, that in case the State had insisted rigorously to go on against him, and forfeit him, they might not get it. But of this there is no certainty; for he had an honourable burial in the sight of several of the nobility and gentry.

His son John, Lord Balmerino,* conquest Crailinghall from his brother-in-law, Sir James Ker, who all his days cried out thereupon, but never got redress. He died in *anno* 1633, that same day that the superiorities of kirk-livings, by act of parliament, were taken from the lords of erection, and made the king's, which he had stoutly opposed during all his life.

At his death he was buried in Restalrig's burial place, being a vaulted isle supported with pillars. And the English army, at their coming to Scotland *in anno* 1650, expecting to have found treasures in that place, hearing that there were lead coffins there, raised up his body and threw it on the street, because they could get no advantage or money where they expected so much; and it is said they vaunted that God made them instruments to punish that cruel fact of his late father, who had raised up the dead body of Restalrig to forfeit it.

The said John, Lord Balmerino, was also indicted of treason by the moyen of the bishops, who then ruled the State; and was de-

* John, second Lord Balmerino, was restored in 1613, his father having died under attainder. Strongly attached to Presbyterianism, he opposed the Act of 1633, imposing apparel upon churchmen. A petition to Charles I. in opposition to the measure, interlined in Balmerino's hand, was, through the treachery of his lawyer, conveyed to the Archbishop of St. Andrews, who, hastening to London, laid it before the King. Sentenced to death as a traitor, he was rescued by the Earl of Traquair, who procured the royal pardon. In 1641 Lord Balmerino was nominated President of Parliament, sworn of the Privy Council, and appointed an extraordinary Lord of Session. He died on the 28th February, 1649.

tained long in the castle of Edinburgh, and condemned to have his head struck off at the cross of Edinburgh, for a paper alleged to have been penned by him prejudicial to his majesty; but King Charles remitted the fault, and restored him to his dignity. He left behind him one son, now lord, who very strangely was kept in life, seeing his mother was near fifty years old before she bore him, and got many potions from doctors, as having a tympany, never imagining she could have a child.

There is a great process in law* depending betwixt the Earl of Bedford, who married his uncle Somerset's only daughter, and him, as heir to his father; and his standing or falling depends on the success of that process.

4. Mr. Thomas Hamilton, son to the good man of Priestfield, was secretary in Balmerino's place. His grandfather was a merchant at the West-bow in Edinburgh.†

---

* His lawsuits resulted in his being compelled to dispose of nearly the whole of his landed property (Anderson's "Scottish Nation").

† Thomas Hamilton, first Earl of Haddington, was eldest son of Sir Thomas Hamilton, of Priestfield, a Lord of Session, and grandson, not of an Edinburgh merchant, but of Thomas Hamilton, of Orchardfield, who fell at the battle of Pinkie. He passed advocate in 1587, and in 1592 became a Lord of Session, under the title of Lord Drumcairn. He was promoted as President of the Court in 1616. In 1595 he was appointed one of the Octavians, or Commissioners of Exchequer, and Lord Advocate in the same year. He was constituted Master of Metals and Minerals in 1607, and Clerk-Register in 1612. The latter office he exchanged for that of Secretary of State. He became opulent to a proverb, having acquired from first to last twenty large estates. In 1613 he was ennobled as Lord Binning and Byres, and in 1619 was elevated to the peerage as Earl of Melrose, a title which he exchanged in 1627 for the earldom of Haddington. On resigning the presidentship and the Secretaryship in 1626, he was appointed Lord Privy Seal. He occupied a stately mansion in the Cowgate of Edinburgh, and was in consequence styled by James VI. "Tam o' the Cowgate." When James visited Scotland in 1619, he remarked to the President that people said he had gained his wealth by possessing the philosopher's stone. "Then it consists," replied the judge, "in these two maxims—never put off till to-morrow what can be done to-day, nor trust to another's hand what your own can execute." Lord Haddington was not more celebrated for his opulence than for his ingenuity and learning. His collection of MSS. and Charters are preserved in the Advocates Library. A portion of them has been printed, in two quarto volumes, by the Bannatyne Club, under the title, "State Papers and Miscellaneous Correspondence of Thomas, Earl of Melros." The Earl died on the 29th May, 1637, in his 74th year (Anderson's "Scottish Nation"; Chambers's "Traditions of Edinburgh").

He was the king's advocate and clerk-register before he was secretary, and one of the Octavians, very learned, but of a choleric constitution. He conquest a great estate. He was first made Earl of Melrose, and then changed his style to Haddington, not choosing to have his title from a kirk-living. He conquest nearly twenty score chalders of victual, for in his lands of Hilderston, near Linlithgow, he got a silver mine, out of which having digged the best part, he then sold it to King James, and got for it £5,000 sterling.

He remained still in great credit till King Charles's time, in that year wherein the king altered the session, and removed therefrom all noblemen, and him among the rest: and he being at court, was challenged by his majesty, that he refused to be president of the council, which the king would have had him accept, and for that cause the king took from him the signet, and gave it to Sir William Alexander, then master of requests, of whom hereafter shall be spoken.

He survived that disaster but few years, and died in good time before he saw the calamities of his house: for his son Thomas, Earl of Haddington, at the beginning of these troubles, being in the house of Dunglass, sent thither by the parliament to have resisted the English incursions, was, by the means of his own chamber-boy, an Englishman, called Dick, with three or four score gentlemen more, miserably murdered, which was done by the firing of a vault full of powder, whereby all the house was blown in the air. With him there died many of his kindred and friends, as Sir John Hamilton of Redhouse, his cousin-german, Sir Alexander Hamilton, younger, of Innerwick, Robert Hamilton, his youngest brother, and Mr. Patrick Hamilton, his bastard brother.*

His eldest son Thomas, having fallen in love with my Lord Chatilion's † daughter in France, married her, and brought her to

---

* Thomas, second Earl of Haddington, was a zealous upholder of the Covenant. When General Leslie, in 1640, proceeded to England, Lord Haddington, being colonel of a regiment, was stationed at Dunglass Castle to watch the garrison at Berwick. On the 30th August, while in the court of the castle he was reading to several gentlemen a letter from General Leslie, the gunpowder magazine exploded, and one of the side walls being blown down, his lordship, with several of his auditors, perished in the ruins. The explosion, it is believed, was the result of an accident, and was not effected by treachery, as our too credulous author has affirmed.

† Thomas, third Earl of Haddington, married in August, 1643, Henrietta de Coligny, eldest daughter of Gaspard, Count de Coligny, a lady afterwards celebrated for her beauty and adventures. The Earl died of consumption in February, 1645, in his seventeenth year.

Scotland, and within half a year after died hectic, and she returned home again. But by these two the house being greatly burdened with debt, his brother John, now Earl of Haddington, has been forced to sell many lands for the relief thereof, as the barony of Luffness, &c.

The first earl's second son, Sir James, had no better success in his affairs: for, in his absence in England with the duke his chief, his lady, the laird of Wauchtoun's daughter, was debauched, and got with child by Mr. Robert Menteith,* now a Jesuit in Paris. The said Sir James had a considerable estate left him by his father, which is all sold and gone.

His third son, Sir John, having gotten in partage the barony of Trabroune, and great sums of money besides, by his riotous living dilapidated all, and he himself died, before his father's death.

His youngest son, Robert, and Mr. Patrick his brother, were smothered at Dunglass.

5. Sir William Alexander, of Menstrie, preferred to be secretary by King Charles, was first brought into court by Prince Henry and respected for his poesy, and the edition of his four tragedies and Doomsday. He travelled through Italy and France, with his lord-superior, the Earl of Argyle, where he attained to the French and Italian tongues.

He got great things from his majesty, as especially, a liberty to create a hundred Scotsmen knights-baronet, from every one of whom he got £200 sterling, or thereby, a liberty to coin base money, far under the value of the weight of copper, which brought great prejudice to the kingdom: at which time he built his great lodgings in Stirling, and put on the gate thereof, *Per mare, per terras*, which a merry man changed, *per metre, per turners;* meaning,

---

* Robert Menteith, styled of Salmonet, was third son of an Edinburgh citizen, and a scion of the ancient house of Menteith. He was some time professor of philosophy in the University of Saumur. In 1630 he was ordained parish minister of Duddingston. Engaging in an illicit amour with the wife of Sir James Hamilton, of Priestfield, he fled the country, and on 7th October, 1633, was denounced rebel. He proceeded to Paris, and having joined the Romish Church, he obtained the patronage of Cardinal Richelieu. By the Cardinal de Retz he was admitted a canon of Notre-Dame. He composed a history of Great Britain in the French tongue, and other works (Dr. Scott's *Fasti*, Edin., 1866, 4to., vol. i. p. 110). The seduced gentlewoman, Dame Anna Hepburn, was remarkable for her personal charms (Harleian MSS., British Museum).

that he had attained to his estate by poesy, and that gift of base money.*

He ventured greatly towards Nova Scotia and America, and sent his eldest son thither, where he lived a winter with three ships. He was of great expectations, and married the Earl of Angus's sister; but his distress and hardships in that voyage procured shortly his death.†

The king also honoured the father with the title of the earldom of Stirling. He got also a great sum of money from the King of France to quit his interest in Nova Scotia; but fell into great distaste with his

---

* William Alexander, afterwards Earl of Stirling, was son of Alexander Alexander, of Menstry. He was born about 1580. His ancestors received the small estate of Menstry from the Earls of Argyle, who remained lords superior of the soil. With Archibald, seventh Earl of Argyle, he travelled in France, Spain, and Italy ("Argyle Papers," p. 19.'; Edin., 1834, 4to.). From his numerous accomplishments, and his skill as a poet, he attracted the notice of James VI., who, on his accession to the English throne, took him to London. He was knighted in 1614, and made Master of Requests. By a charter dated 10th September, 1621, he obtained a grant of the territory of Nova Scotia. He was authorized to divide the lands into one hundred parcels, and dispose of them, along with the title of baronet. The privilege of issuing a coin of base metal was granted him. He was appointed Secretary of State in 1626, Keeper of the signet in 1627, a Commissioner of Exchequer in 1628, and an extraordinary Judge of the Court of Session in 1631. Having been raised to the peerage, he was created Earl of Stirling in June, 1633. He died at London in February, 1640. Sir William Alexander, Sir Robert Aytoun, and William Drummond, of Hawthornden, were the first Scottish poets who composed in English verse. In 1603 Alexander made his first poetical adventure by publishing at Edinburgh his "Tragedie of Darius," with a dedication to King James. In the following year he published at London "Aurora, containing the first fancies of the Author's youth," a collection of love sonnets, sextains, &c., dedicated to the Countess of Argyle. In 1607 he issued his "Monarchiche Tragedies." His "Recreations of the Muses," his latest poetical work, appeared in 1637. A collected edition of his "Poetical Works" is now in course of publication at Glasgow, to be completed in three elegant duodecimo volumes.

† Sir William Alexander, the younger, landed at Port Royal in 1629, and there remained till the following year. He effected a straggling settlement, and erected a fort on the west side of the haven (Granville), nearly opposite to Goat Island. But thirty of the Scottish settlers died during the winter, and proved a considerable discouragement (Preface by David Laing, LL.D., to the Earl of Stirling's Royal Letters, p. 98). Sir William Alexander the younger, on his father's elevation to the earldom of Stirling, assumed the courtesy title of Lord Alexander and Viscount Canada. He married Lady Margaret Douglas, eldest daughter of William, first Marquis of Douglas. He pre-deceased his father, having died at London on the 18th May, 1638 ("Earl of Stirling's Register" in the Advocates Library).

country; for his affection was carried towards the bishops, and the maintaining their cause.

He conquest, to his old heritage of Menstrie, the baronies of Tillicultrie and Gogar; all which were comprised from his heirs instantly after his decease; and of six or seven sons, none but one or two are remaining.* The house of Menstrie was burnt by command of his superior, the Earl of Argyle, because his sons were favourers of James Graham and his party.

6. Sir Archibald Acheson, of Glencairny, conjunct secretary with the said Earl of Stirling, enjoyed the place but few years, and had no land in Scotland, but some four hundred pounds sterling in Ireland of the Earl of Tyrone's lands. His eldest son was of great expectation, having married a rich heiress in England. He died the first year of their marriage without issue.

Of his second wife, Sir William Hamilton's daughter, he had but one son, George; but his mother turned Papist after Sir Archibald's death, and said she had ventured her soul for an *Acheson*. He died of a pestilential fever; and it is thought that his son George shall get nothing of that estate, it being all destroyed by war in the late troubles.†

---

* The Earl of Stirling was father of eight sons; William, afterwards Viscount Canada; Anthony, knighted at Whitehall 10th January, 1635, died 17th September, 1637; Henry, third earl, died August, 1644; John, died before 1645; Charles, Robert, died young; Ludovick, died before 1640; and James. Charles was eldest surviving son in 1645. James had a daughter baptized at Edinburgh in June, 1669 (Edinburgh Baptismal Register).

† Archibald Acheson, of Gosport, in the county of Haddington, obtained in 1611 a large grant of lands in the county of Armagh, and in the following year additional lands in the county of Cavan. In January, 1628, he was created a Baronet of Nova Scotia. He was successively Solicitor-General, a senator of the College of Justice, and conjunct Secretary of State for Scotland. He possessed a large and elegant mansion in the Canongate of Edinburgh, which still remains, presenting over the doorway a crest representing a cock mounted on a trumpet, with the motto, VIGILANTIBUS, and the date 1633. Over two upper windows are the letters S. A. A. and D. M. H., the initials of Sir Archibald and his wife Dame Margaret Hamilton (Chambers's "Traditions of Edinburgh"). Sir Archibald died at Letterkenny, county Donegal, Ireland, in 1634. He had two sons, Patrick, who succeeded him, and died in 1638, *s. p.*, and George, third baronet, and owner of the Irish estates when our author composed his work. A descendant and representative of the House was landlord of Swift at Market Hill, and is celebrated by the Dean in several of his poems. The Dean styles the baronet *Skinni-*

7. Sir Robert Spottiswood, second son to the Bishop of St. Andrews, and President of the College of Justice, having fled out of Scotland after the extermination of the bishops, attended on the court at Oxford, where being resident in 1644 (at that time when the Lord Lanark, prisoner in Oxford, by the means of Robert Land's brother, was carried out disguised in habit as his footman, through all the guards, and brought home to Scotland), had the favour of the king to be substituted in the said Lord Lanark's place, and made Secretary of Scotland, and got presently delivered to him the signet, wherewith all papers that passed that office were stamped, which signet he had in his pocket when he was sent home by his majesty to make friendship betwixt the Hamiltons and James Graham, that they might concur together to suppress the alleged rebellion of the subjects there; but being taken prisoner at Philiphaugh, he was condemned for treason by the Parliament of St. Andrews, *in anno* 1645, and beheaded there, and the signet given back to the said Earl of Arran.*

8. William, Earl of Lanark, only brother to James, Marquis of Hamilton, Secretary for some years; in whose person, seeing that family is likely to end, it seems not unfit here shortly to set down, as well what is recorded of them in history as what has happened since remarkable among them.

---

bonia, Lean, or *Snipe,* as his humour moved him. In one of his poems he thus refers to the Scottish Secretary:—

> "Sir Archibald, that valorous knight,
> The lord of all the fruitful plain,
> Would come and listen with delight,
> For he was fond of rural strain :
>
> "Sir Archibald, whose favourite name
> Shall stand for ages on record,
> By Scottish bards of highest fame,
> Wise Hawthornden and Stirling's lord."

The great-grandson of the Secretary was created Earl of Gosford in 1806, and the earl's grandson was in 1847 raised to the British peerage as Baron Acheson.

* Sir Robert Spottiswood was an eminent lawyer, and author of "The Practicks of the Law of Scotland." He was appointed President of the Court of Session in November, 1633. On account of his strong attachment to Episcopacy, he was in 1637 obliged to retire into England. In 1645 he was appointed by Charles I. Secretary of State for Scotland.

It had its beginning in the time of K. Robert Bruce, and the first of that name * fled from England for killing one of the Spensers, a favourite of the King of England, of whom before he had been wounded for praising the valour of the said king. The said Robert Bruce bestowed on him many lands in Clydesdale, which he entitled Hamilton, after his name. Thereafter he got sundry lands from the Earl of Douglas, and became his follower,† and was sent by him, in King James II.'s time, after the killing of his brother in Stirling with the king's own hand, for refusing to break the league betwixt the Earls of Crawfurd and Ross,‡ back to Stirling, after the said earl had caused trail the king's great seal at a horse's tail through the town, and from him got orders to burn the said town, which he did.

Then was he sent by the said earl to England, to incite the king to raise war against Scotland, who refused, except the earl would acknowledge himself to be a subject of England; and at his return, he gave council to the said earl to fight a battle with the king, and either there to win honestly, or die gloriously. And because the earl was unwilling to put all to the hazard of one battle, at the raising of the siege of Abercorn, he left the said earl's part, and went in to the king; thus betraying his friend and benefactor.§

* Some authors call him Gilbert Hamilton, but Buchanan, who tells the story, does not mention his name; he says, only, that his posterity having attained to a high degree, gave their name to their lands. (*Vide* "Buch. Hist.," lib. 8, sec. 49.) And neither the men nor the lands seem to have borne the name of Hamilton for very many years after Robert Bruce's death.—*Goodal.*

† This gentleman's name was James Hamilton of Cadyow, Kt.—*Goodal.*

‡ This was a league entered into by them, offensive and defensive, against all the world, to the friends and confederates of each other; and Douglas being very obnoxious for his other lawless actions, King James II., at a private interview with him in the castle of Stirling, in February, 1452, intreated him, among other things, to dissolve this league, which Douglas refusing, the king, thereat exasperated, replied, "If you will not break it I will," and immediately killed him.—*Goodal.*

§ This behaviour of the Hamiltons is by some imputed to the secret management of that wise and good prelate, Bishop Kennedy, who had allured him with the promise, not only of his remission, but of the king's favour, if he would leave Douglas's party. Others allege that Hamilton, upon Douglas delaying to fight the king's army when they offered, imputed it to cowardice, or to a design to protract the war; and, after expostulating with him, carried off his men and joined the king, and the rest followed his example, so that Douglas and the friends who adhered to him were forced to fly, and retire to England.—*Goodal.*

They became great by the fall of the Boyds, in 1470. For Robert, Lord Boyd,* being forfeited for alleged taking away the king, James III., from the Exchequer in Linlithgow, and carrying him to Edinburgh contrary to his will (whereof he had a fair approbation in parliament as good service, but wanted the extract of the same, when challenged for it, and could not get it out of the register, by reason of the power of his enemies, albeit at this day it stands therein),† his brother, Mr. Alexander, was headed in Edinburgh, my lord himself fled to England, and there died. His son, Thomas, Lord Boyd,‡ being then ambassador in Denmark, and having to his wife the king's eldest sister,§ not daring to return for fear of his life, and coming near land, was persuaded by her to go back; whom she accompanied, and staid divers years in Flanders, till some from her brother persuaded her that she could be the only person that could make friendship. In that hope she being sent home to Scotland, was urged by the king her brother to quit him, after they had caused cite him upon sixty days to adhere, and for his contumacy recovering a decreet of divorcement, forced his said sister to marry James Hamilton,‖ and gave him the Isle of Arran,¶ and many lands which pertained to the said Lord Boyd.

* Buchanan says that Robert, Lord Boyd, was Chancellor, but Mr. Crawfurd, in his lives of the Officers of State, alleges, from apparently good reasons, that he never was Chancellor, and that Andrew Stewart, Lord Evandale, was Chancellor at this period.—*Goodal.*

† The king of his own accord declared in Parliament that, what Lord Boyd had done was not of himself, but at the king's own desire, and what he esteemed good service, and more worthy of reward than censure, which he offered to confirm by a decree of the States, which was immediately made, and registered on the 18th of October, 1468, and an extract made out, and confirmed by letters patent under the Great Seal. It is not clear upon what account this pardon did not operate an absolvitor to the Boyds; whether it was owing to their being refused an extract, or the privilege of the record on the trial, and so could not plead it before the Parliament, or that it was pleaded and judged ineffectual. Buchanan insinuates the last, and imputes it to an evasive distinction suggested by priestcraft. (Buch. Hist. lib. 12, sec. 29.)—*Goodal.*

‡ He was then Earl of Arran.

§ Her name was Mary Stuart.

‖ This was the son of that James Hamilton of Cadyow, Kt., who deserted the Earl of Douglas. He was at this time styled Lord Hamilton. Some allege Boyd was dead before that marriage.—*Goodal.*

¶ He did not get Arran till the year 1503, and was then made Lord Arran.—*Goodal.*

James, Earl of Arran, in hatred of the Douglasses, whose followers they had been of old, having assisted the Laird of Fernihirst against them *in anno* 1517, came to Edinburgh, and there invading the Earl of Angus in the streets, was beaten and forced to fly over the North-loch, having had his brother killed with seventy-two more.*

Yet was his friendship so inconsistent, that in 1526, after the said Earl of Angus's return from France, being then hated of the queen, his wife, mother to King James V., the Lord Hamilton agreed with the said Earl of Angus, and entered in strict friendship, that they two † might keep King James V. in their power till his majority; whereat the young king being grieved exceedingly, wrote to the Laird of Buccleuch to relieve him out of their hands; whereupon followed the battle of Melrose, where the Laird of Cessford, one of the Douglasses party, was killed.

Thereafter, when the Earl of Lennox, at the king's command, gathered the nobility to Stirling, and was coming to Edinburgh to relieve the king, the Hamiltons joined with the Douglasses at Linlithgow, and killed the said Earl of Lennox,‡ who was his own sister's son.

After that field of Linlithgow, the Earl of Arran having summoned the Earl of Cassilis before the justice, for being at the field against the king, and yet underhand having sent him word, that if he would give him his bond of Manrent, he should be absolved; and the said earl having sent him back word,§ that in a bond of mutual friendship made betwixt their forefathers, the Earl of Cassilis was first placed

---

* This happened on the 30th of April, 1520, according to Buchanan; but Pitscottie says it was in May, 1515.—*Goodal.*

† They were not the only persons, for Argyle and Lennox were conjoined with them, and all four declared tutors and guardians of the king and the realm. But the Earl of Angus soon assumed the whole power into his own hands, and ruled the king as he pleased.—*Goodal.*

‡ He was killed by James Hamilton, bastard son to the Earl of Arran, and it is said in cold blood, after he was taken, much wounded, and in the custody of the Laird of Pardovan.—*Goodal.*

§ The Earl of Cassilis's answer, which is very lamely told by our author, was that, as in the old league betwixt their families, his family had always had the preference, and was first named, he would not so far degenerate from the glory of his ancestors, as to come under the patronage of a family, whose chief, in an equal alliance, had been content with the second place.—*Goodal.*

in the writ, and that he had the king's own hand-writ for his being at that field; he was thereupon for that time dismissed. But in his going home, he was treacherously murdered by the Sheriff of Ayr by the council of James Hamilton, the earl's bastard son. Wherein may appear the notable ingratitude of that family to the house of Cassilis, whose predecessor, in King James III.'s time, was the author of the Boyds' forfeiture, and of bringing them into court, only upon that reason, that Alexander Boyd, the king's teacher, and lord's brother, broke Bishop Kennedy's head at Linlithgow with a bow.

They strove what in them lay to impede the king's marriage with France, and hindered the conference craved by Henry VIII., the King's uncle, with James V., wherein was offered his daughter in marriage, and to make him King of all the isle of Britain, and presently to make him Duke of York, and so next person to the Crown.*

The said King James V., being reconciled with James, Lord Hamilton, who slew the Earl of Lennox, he took him with him to France when he went to seek his wife; and having been overtaken at sea with a storm, the said James counselled the mariners to take the king back again to Scotland when he was asleep, wherewith he was grievously offended.

James Hamilton, the Earl of Arran's base brother, who was in extreme great credit with King James V., and from him got new arms given him by the king's patent, yet standing in the register, being accused by James Hamilton, Sheriff of Linlithgow, of certain crimes, namely, that he on a certain day was to break up the king's chamber, and there to have murdered him, was for that offence beheaded in Edinburgh, and his quarters put on divers parts of the town.

When the nobility and the estates had placed the Earl of Arran in the room of Cardinal Beaton, who, by a counterfeit testament,† had got himself made tutor to the queen, he professed himself to be a

---

* The family of Hamilton were strongly induced to this by the hopes of their succession to the crown, being nearest heirs, failing heirs of King James V., as descended of Mary, sister to James III.—*Goodal.*

† See the history of this testament, as related by Pitscottie, p. 323 of his History, which is very different from what Buchanan says of it, *lib.* 15, of his hist. *ab initio*, and in his admonition to the true lords, &c., p. 16, where he expressly calls it a forged deed or instrument.—*Goodal.*

lover of the reformed religion; his government not as yet, says Buchanan, kything the dulness and sottishness of his engine.*

Eight days after K. James V.'s death, the Earl of Arran having convened the nobility, in that meeting the cardinal and his faction opposed him, and did dispute against the government and sovereignty of one man, and especially of any called Hamilton. For who knows not, said he, that the Hamiltons are cruel murderers, oppressors of innocents, cruel and false, and finally the pestilence of the commonwealth? Whereunto the earl answered, "Defraud me not of my right, and call me what you please; whatsoever my friends have done, yet none has cause to complain of me."

Buchanan and Knox both agree that that James Hamilton the viceroy was a bastard, and by law could neither have right to the heritage of that family, nor title to the crown. For his father's first married wife was Elizabeth Home, sister to the Lord Home. His second wife was of the name of Beaton, niece to James, Bishop of St. Andrews, whom he married, the said Elizabeth being yet in life; and his grandfather was the son of Mary Stuart, who bore him when her lawful husband, Thomas Lord Boyd, was yet in life.

By evil counsel he refused to deliver to the English ambassador the pledges promised to the kingdom of England,† and supppressed

* Buchanan's words are, *Ipse quoque libellos, qui controversias de religione continebant, libenter lectitabat, & vitæ superioris quies, procul ab aulica ambitione remota, spem animi modesti & temperantis multis faciebat, magistratu nondum torporem & socordiam ingenii detegente, lib.* 15. But what credit should be given to Buchanan (whom our author follows for the most part implicitly) in what he says of this family of Hamilton, may be judged from what another historian has recorded of him; "That being provoked by an injury which a servant of the Duke of Chatelrault's youngest son did him, of which he thought he got not sufficient reparation, and carrying a spite to them, because he thought they adhered to the queen's interest, he wrote of that family with the most impudent and virulent malice that was possible" (Bishop Burnet, in the Preface to his "Memoirs of the Dukes of Hamilton").—*Goodal.*

† In the year 1543 a treaty had been concluded with England, for the marriage of the son of Henry VIII. with Queen Mary, then a child, and hostages were agreed to be delivered for security of the performance. This treaty was vigorously opposed by Cardinal Beaton and the queen-mother, and such commotion afterwards raised by their intrigues as put it out of the regent's power to deliver the hostages as stipulated. This, and the personal affronts offered to the English ambassador, occasioned a war betwixt the two nations, which lasted a considerable while, during which the battle of Pinkie was fought, in September, 1547, and the English possessed Haddington, and many of the forts in the country, till the year 1549.—*Goodal.*

a letter, then sent by the governor of the English army, desiring only that their young queen should not be contracted in marriage to any foreign prince, till she was of age to give her own consent thereto; whereupon followed that unhappy field of Pinkie, wherein was shed so much Scots blood.

The said governor, after the Earl of Lennox's home-coming to Scotland in hopes of marrying the queen-regent, to oppose him and strengthen his own faction, stirred up the Earl of Bothwell to be a suitor to the queen-regent, and openly himself changed his religion in the Greyfriars kirk.

He caused strike off the head of the laird of Raith, by the counsel of the bishops, only for writing a letter to an Englishman, recommending a friend to him; and having forfeited him, gave his lands to David, his youngest son.*

When he agreed with the King of France to quit the government to the queen-regent, he swore solemnly that he should render to her all the household stuff belonging to King James V.; yet twelve years after that, at the field of Langside, there was much of the same stuff found in his house, proving his perjury.†

The Earl of Bothwell having offered to my Lord Arran to kill James, Earl of Murray,‡ the governor's son revealed it to Murray, for which his father imprisoned him, and for grief thereof he became furious.

After the queen's marriage with Lord Darnley,—Hamilton, Argyle, Murray, Glencairn, and Rothes, to show their discontent thereat, went all to Argyle; at which time the king and queen went west to cast down Hamilton; and the Lord Hamilton's friends, advising what was fit to be done, concluded that both king and queen behoved to be killed, and put off the way, or else, said he, "there will never be peace:" telling them that injuries done to princes were only ex-

---

* See *supra*.

† The charge of perjury rests on the authority of Buchanan.

‡ Let the reader compare Buchanan's Hist., *lib.* 19, § 29, and his Admonition, &c. with Knox's Hist., lib. 4, p. 308, and he will perceive how unjust this charge is. Knox, who, from the account he gives of it, appears to have had much greater access to know the matter than Buchanan, ascribes the whole to a wild fancy in the frantic head of the Earl of Arran; and says that he himself advised the Earl of Murray to lay no great stress to it; and that his opinion was confirmed by Arran's frenzy increasing, during which he declared that he was enchanted so to think and write.—*Goodal.*

tinguished by their deaths. But Murray and Glencairn, knowing that that was spoken for his own interest, he being nearest to the crown, abhorred so bloody a counsel, and opposed it.

When the queen was informed that the Lord Darnley, her husband, intended to fly to France or Spain, and a ship lying ready at the mouth of Clyde, she with the Lord Hamilton and his friends, went to Glasgow to hinder his flight, and when they made him condescend to go back to Edinburgh, there he was strangled by Bothwell in the kirk of field, the Bishop of St. Andrews being in his brother's lodging hard by, which now is the College of Edinburgh; and so soon as the blow was given it was remarked that the lights were put out, and they went to bed: in which lodging the bishop was never accustomed to dwell before, but in the town.*

By the said earl's command and direction the Earl of Murray was killed in Linlithgow by David Hamilton of Bothwellhaugh, who before was condemned for treason and pardoned by the said earl.†

Anno 1571, the queen's faction made the raid of Stirling; there they took the hail nobility who were of the king's party in their beds. One of the chief leaders was David Hamilton, whose counsel was, that all the noblemen should be killed so soon as they were out of the ports;‡ but by sixteen musketeers of the Earl of Mar's that went into the new work, standing in the head of the market-place, they were all chased out of the town; and many surrendered themselves to them who before were their prisoners. In this conflict the Earl of Lennox was murdered in cold blood. §

The said James, Earl of Arran, then styled Duke of Chatelrault,

* Buchanan.

† James, not David Hamilton, of Bothwellhaugh, was excited to hostility against the Regent Murray on account of severities with which he had been visited by the latter for having fought in the cause of Queen Mary at Langside. The accusation preferred against the Earl of Arran, in connexion with the regent's death, seems to be entirely unfounded.

‡ This is very improbable. Sir James Melvil, in his Memoirs, p. 217, says expressly that they had all engaged, before they left Edinburgh, not to kill one man.—*Goodal.*

§ Lennox had surrendered, and was in the custody of Sir David Spence, when the party were surprised by Mar's musketeers, and obliged to fly and abandon their victory; and in this confusion he was wounded by some of them, no doubt out of rage and disappointment. Spence endeavoured to save him, but to no purpose, and he himself was immediately cut to pieces.—*Goodal.*

died in *anno* 1579, in Poictiers,* and left four sons, James, Earl of Arran, John, Claude, and David. The last three were all frantic, † as many since of that family have been, viz., Edward Maxwell, son to Elspeth Hamilton, a daughter of Innerwick's, who, for striking of Archibald Hamilton at the board with a whinger, alleging that he saw the devil in him, lay many years in bonds in his own house of Maulslie, and his brother, Sir James, got the lands totally dilapidated. The Lord Evandale, who leaped in a hot limekiln, and said, if hell was no hotter he would endure it. Francis Hamilton, brother to the late Earl of Abercorn, having been furious at his majority, died in the Chartreuse-monks monastery at Paris. And that Lord Abercorn's sister's grandson, the Lord Seton, the first night of his marriage threw a chamber-pot in his wife's bosom, and lay in fetters till he died; and Sir William Seton, of the same degree with the former, would needs have the sword from the king wherewith he knighted him, and has still been frantic since. Also Alexander Hamilton, son to Sir John of Ettrick, a bastard of the house, his son, now Lord Bargeny's brother, was mad. And Francis Hamiiton, son to Silverton-hill, lineally descended of that house lived long distracted in Edinburgh, ever complaining in judicatories that a lady had bewitched him, and never recovered thereof till he died of the pest in Edinburgh.

The secretary's grandfather, the first Marquis of Hamilton, respected much Sir John of Ettrick, his base son, and was so charitable to all the bastards of that family, and all others who alleged themselves to be descended of them, that, when any woman brought a child to the gates, he directed them to place them in his kitchen, and call them all Hamiltons in the devil's name.

James, Marquis of Hamilton, the secretary's father, lived all his time in England, and by King James was once employed as viceroy to a parliament in 1621, which is yet called the Black Parliament. For at the conclusion and rising of the same by the three estates, such a horrible tempest and thunder fell in the midst of summer,

* Crawfurd states that he died at his own palace of Hamilton on the 22nd January, 1575.

† James, the eldest son, was insane, and after the forfeiture of his brethren, Captain James Stewart was made his tutor. And notwithstanding his being mad, he also was soon after forfeited by Morton, and his estate, together with the title of Earl of Arran, given to Captain Stewart, who afterwards became chancellor.—*Goodal.*

that the like was never seen.* In his middle age he was poisoned by a lady whom he had slighted.

He it was that had the chief hand in begging from the king all the kirk-livings in 1606, which were annexed to the crown before in 1587, whereby the crown lost a third of its rents; and he and his friends got among them Aberbrothoc, Paisley, Manuel, Bothwell, Haddington, Melrose, and Lesmahago.

He married his base sister to John Hamilton, whom he procured to be made Lord Belhaven, who, in *anno* 1653, was swallowed up in Solway sands, horse and all, and never seen again.

The secretary's eldest brother, James, Marquis of Hamilton, was in as great favour with King Charles as his father was with King James, and was master of his horses, and a chief counsellor. It was he who advised the king to grant to the estates of England triennial parliaments, and the militia.

He got from the king a grant of the customs of Scotland for divers years, contrary to the laws, being of great value; † and also a gift of two of the hundred, whereby, by causing dash out a word, *free*, by Sir John Hay, Clerk-Register, in the first printed Act, he evicted from the subjects above 800,000 merks Scots; for no lent money in the kingdom was free from payment of that two in the hundred, albeit the meaning of the estates in making the said Act was, that only free money should pay, the owners thereof not being addebted in sums of money to others; I say, such only should have paid two of the hundred, which infinitely harmed the lieges. ‡

* This was the 4th August, 1621. It was interpreted by the Puritans as a visible sign of God's anger, for ratifying the five articles concluded in the Assembly at Perth.—*Goodal.*

† James, second Marquis of Hamilton, died at Whitehall, London, on the 2nd March, 1625, at the age of thirty-six. The Duke of Buckingham, with whom he was at variance, was reported to have poisoned him, and his body being examined by three physicians, two declared that there were no traces of poison, while a third, Dr. Eglisham, maintained that there were, and ascribed the crime to Buckingham. For this expression of his opinion he was obliged to seek refuge in Flanders.

‡ The author is much mistaken in his account of this matter. For, 1st, the marquis had not the gift of the customs, and that of the two pounds in the hundred, or more properly two pounds of ten of the annual rents then by law payable for £100 of principal, both at one time: for the king, when in Scotland in 1633, being informed by Traquair, then treasurer-depute, that these customs were the readiest and surest money the king had, and that the treasury would signify little without

He was most unfortunate in his foreign expeditions; for being sent to Germany with an army by the king, he lost the same totally by pest and famine.* No better success had his naval army that was sent against Scotland in 1638.† His last expedition was the worst of all, viz., the unhappy engagement against England, which, by his friendship and led votes, he carried through parliament, contrary to the will of the honest party; which has been the chief ground of the English invasion, and overthrow of this land; and being leader in chief of that powerful army at Preston, was defeated by a small number of English; and when the king heard by Mr. Halyburton that he was leader of the forces, he said he would never get good by him, seeing he was unfortunate; and though after his imprisonment

---

them, was prevailed on to cause the marquis exchange them for the other, to reimburse him of the charge he had been at in his German expedition. 2ndly, the fraud imputed to the marquis and the Clerk-Register seems without foundation; for it appears from the printed Act imposing this duty, that the legal interest which at that time was 10 per cent, was reduced to 8, but not to take place for three years; and thereby neither the borrower nor the lender was hurt, the first being only for three years kept from the benefit which he was thereafter to enjoy, and in the meantime paid no more than he was formerly obliged to; and the lender got what the wisdom of the nation thought sufficient for the use of his money. And the marquis afterwards accounting for the surplus to the Lords of Exchequer and Session, after discounting his own claims, removes all suspicion of this sort."—*Goodal.*

* The Elector Palatine, who married K. Charles's sister, having been elected King of Bohemia, was soon dispossessed of his royalty by the House of Austria, and had applied to K. James, and, after his death, to K. Charles, for assistance. But as he did not think it convenient for himself to appear openly in the cause, he pitched upon the Marquis of Hamilton, who warmly espoused the prince's quarrel, to levy forces within the kingdom as of himself; which in summer, 1631, he carried to Germany, to the number of 6,000, and joined Gustavus Adolphus of Sweden, who supported the interest of the Palatine. But that part of the country which had been the seat of the war was entirely wasted, and provisions very scarce; and the plague having also attacked his small army, it was soon totally ruined: and having got no new supply, nor being properly supported by the King of Sweden, he relinquished that enterprise, and returned, bringing few or none back with him.—*Goodal.*

† This was in the beginning of the war between the King and the Covenanters. The Covenanters having first commenced hostilities, the king came down to York with an army by land, and, at the same time, the marquis came down to the Frith with a fleet and 5,000 men, and he continued there till he went to attend the king then near Berwick, where a pacification was concluded.—*Goodal.*

at London he had escaped, yet was he again taken,* arraigned as an English nobleman, and beheaded at Westminster,† a year or two after he was made duke ;‡ which title, Buchanan says, is fatal to all Scotsmen.

His brother Lord William, thereafter styled Earl of Lanark, was secretary from the death of the Earl of Stirling till he was thrust out by the parliament for the cause of the engagement ;§ and had so great credit with the king his master, that he obtained a warrant to all the writers of seals, director of the chancellary, and chancellor, not to suffer anything to pass their hands, which was not attested by him as well as the king.

He returned from Holland when King Charles II. came home to get the crown, and had so great respect with him, that he moved all the churchmen, the General Assembly and statesmen, to accept of him as a special convert ; and so accompanying his Majesty with his army to Worcester, he was there grievously wounded, of which he shortly thereafter died.‖

9. Sir William Ker, the only son of Sir Robert Ker of Ancrum, by his father's means and credit at court, being a gentleman of King James VI.'s bedchamber, with the help and assistance of his cousin

* He had escaped from Windsor, where he was imprisoned, but was taken again that same night in Southwark.—*Goodal.*

† He was arraigned as Earl of Cambridge (which title had been conferred upon his father by King James) for invading England in a hostile manner, and levying war to assist the king against the kingdom and people of England. And though the defence which he pleaded was certainly good, viz., that he had acted at the command and by the authority of the Parliament of Scotland, of which nation he was born a subject before his father's naturalization in England, and so an alien of that kingdom, and not triable there, and that he had surrendered to Lambert upon a capitulation, whereby his life was secured ; he was notwithstanding condemned, and was beheaded, 9th March, 1648-9.—*Goodal.*

‡ He was created a duke in 1643.—*Goodal.*

§ He was made secretary in the year 1640, when he was but twenty-four years of age, and in the year 1641 was confirmed in that office by the parliament, when they resolved that the king should employ none as officers of state without their consent. He continued till the year 1644, when he and his brother, the duke, were imprisoned at Oxford on account of the jealousies then entertained of them ; at which time Sir Robert Spottiswood was appointed by the king. After Sir Robert's execution, he was replaced again by the parliament, and continued till he was turned out by them for his concern in the engagement, which then went under the name of THE UNLAWFUL ENGAGEMENT.—*Goodal.*

‖ 12th September, 1652.

the Earl of Somerset, minion to King James, from goodman of Ancrum attained to the marriage of the eldest daughter of the house of Lothian, and thereafter to be secretary when the Earl of Lanark fell ; and was expelled for malignancy.

His grandfather William Ker was shot in Edinburgh behind his back by the late Earl of Roxburgh, when he was a young man, and laird of Cessford, for some private quarrel ;* and his father Sir Robert was thereafter made Earl of Ancrum, at King Charles I.'s coming to Scotland, in 1633, who being provoked to combat by Charles Maxwell, brother to James Maxwell, gentleman usher, killed the said Charles at the market-fields, and behoved to go to Holland till he was reconciled to the party, and then returned to his place, and got a remission, and married the Earl of Derby's sister, who for assisting Charles II. was beheaded at Bolton, the 15th of October, 1651.

That heretrix of Lothian, whom Sir William married, was eldest daughter to Robert, Earl of Lothian, eldest son to Mark, commendator of Newbottle, a cadet of the house of Cessford,† who got that abbacy erected into a temporal lordship by King James VI. about the time of his going to England. And the father and son did so metamorphose the buildings, that it cannot be known that ever it did belong to the church, by reason of the fair new fabric and stately edifices built thereon ; except only that the old name and walls of

---

* There had been a long and old emulation betwixt the two families of Cessford and Fernihirst, for the Wardenship of the Middle Marches, and the Provostry of Jedburgh. But Fernihirst being then deceased, and the heir left young, this gentleman, William Ker of Ancrum, as descended of that house, did what he could to maintain the reputation of it, which was an eyesore to the other. And some time before, this gentleman, in the trial of goods stolen from England, was so vigilant as to discover the thief, who was one of Cessford's followers, and, when it was denied, to bring clear testimony of it before the council ; which was taken to be done out of spleen, and to rub some infamy upon Cessford, who was then warden. This the Lady Cessford, a woman of a haughty spirit, highly resented, and moved her son, then very young, to murder Ancrum, which he did in the year 1591. His death was much lamented, he being a wise and courageous gentleman, and expert beyond most men in the laws and customs of the borders ; which, and the manner of his death, exasperated the king, who resolved to use exemplary justice on the actor. But he having escaped, after some months' absence, was pardoned, upon satisfaction made to Ancrum's children, and as was thought by the intercession of Chancellor Maitland, who afterwards married him to his niece, a daughter of William Maitland, the secretary.—*Goodal.*

† It should be Fernihirst.

the precinct stands; but instead of the old monks has succeeded the deer.

The said Mark, the lady's grandfather, was master of requests to King James VI.,* and had by his wife, the Lord Herries's sister, thirty-one children; and, not satisfied with her, was much inclined to lasciviousness, and was not free of the crime of adultery. His lady kept always in her company wise women, or witches, and especially one Margaret Nues (F. *Innes*), who fostered his daughter, the Lady Borthwick, who was long after his death burnt in Edinburgh for that crime; and my Lady Lothian's son-in-law, Sir Alexander Hamilton, told one of his friends, how one night lying in Prestongrange, pertaining to the said abbacy of Newbottle, he was pulled out of his bed by the said witches, and sore beaten; of which injury when he complained to his mother-in-law, and assured her he would complain thereof to the council, she pacified him by giving him a purse-full of gold. That lady thereafter, being vexed with a cancer in her breast, implored the help of a notable warlock, by a by-name called Playfair, who condescended to heal her, but with condition that the sore should fall on them that she loved best; whereunto she agreeing did convalesce, but the Earl her husband found the boil in his throat, of which he died shortly thereafter; and the said Playfair, being soon apprehended, was made prisoner in Dalkeith steeple, and having confessed that and much more wickedness to Mr. Archibald Simson, minister there, and that confession coming to the ears of Robert, Earl of Lothian, my lord's son, he had moyen to get some persons admitted to speak with the prisoner in the night, by which means he was found worried in the morning, and the point of his breeches knit about his neck; but never more inquiry was made who had done the deed.

The said Robert, Earl of Lothian, father-in-law to the said secretary, married the Marquis of Argyle's sister, a woman of a masculine spirit, but highland-faced; yet so much given to her own contentment, that she kept in the house a young gentleman called William Douglas of Tofts, the grandson of James, Earl of Morton, a man of a brave personage, and of a notable spirit; which was very scandalous, and much talked of in the country; especially seeing her husband the said Earl, in a morning, was found lying in his own

* From 1578 to 1597.

chamber with his throat cut, never man knowing who was the author of that wicked deed.

By his decease his eldest daughter attained to the right of the earldom, and, by her, her husband the said Sir William. Her other sister shortly thereafter left the kingdom, being much slandered for incontinency, and is now in Holland in a boor's house, teaching children.

The lady her mother went to France a few years after her husband's death, where she yet lives ; and the said William Douglas to Holland, where shortly thereafter he was killed at a siege.

This Earl of Lothian was colonel of a regiment, which was totally defeated by James Graham at Aulderne, and many of his kindred and friends there perished.*

He was sent by the estates of Scotland to France to seek help there, and, at his return, was imprisoned by King Charles in Pendennis Castle, but was relieved by the credit of the Earl of Traquair, and got leave to return to Scotland.

His next voyage was to bring home Charles II., with others of the nobility ; whose return has not had the success expected by the kingdom of Scotland. Since which time, three others of the domestic servants of that family have put violent hands to themselves by hanging ; two in the month of March, and the last in May, 1662. The last of them, called Andrew Learmont, was servant to young Sir William, my lord's second son.

Lords Privy Seal.

1. Sir Richard Maitland, of Lethington, was keeper of the Privy Seal in the queen regent's time, and a counsellor and Lord of the Session.†

* May, 1645.

† Sir Richard Maitland was born in 1496 ; he studied philosophy at St. Andrews, and law in France. After occupying different public offices about the court, he was, in March, 1551, appointed an extraordinary Lord of Session, and ten years afterwards a lord ordinary, by the title of Lord Lethington. In December, 1562, he was nominated Lord Privy Seal, but resigned the office in 1567 in favour of his second son, John, afterwards Lord Maitland, of Thirlestane. He resigned his seat on the bench in 1584 in favour of Sir Lewis Bellenden, of Auchnoull. He died on the 20th March, 1586, aged ninety. For nearly thirty years he was afflicted with blindness. He collected the Decisions of the Court of Session, made a valuable collection of ancient Scottish poetry, and composed a history of the House of Seton. The last work and his own poems have been printed for the Bannatyne Club.

He is highly taxed by Knox in his chronicle, for taking a sum of money to let loose the cardinal, when he was prisoner at Seton.*

He lived to a good age in these places, and what success his family had will be found in the life of Chancellor Maitland, who, being tutor to his brother's son, James Maitland, because he was a Papist, got the right to his lands.

2. Mr. George Buchanan was instructor in learning to King James VI. in his youth. He is so renowned by his works extant to the world in prose and verse, that it were superfluous to speak or write anything of him in this catalogue of statesmen.

For the reward of his good services, he got first the office of Director of the Chancellary, and then was made Keeper of the Privy Seal in his old age; but of both these places he reaped little or no advantage. He left neither lands nor sums of money to his successors. He was never married.

He was in so great disgust with the State before he died, that they caused summon him before them sitting in council, for some passages too plain in his chronicle of the king's mother and grandmother; and he had undoubtedly run greater hazard of his life, if the Lord had not freed him from the miseries of this world betwixt the citation and the day of his compearance. He told the messenger who summoned him, he was to compear before a higher judge, which so fell out. Yet was his chronicle prohibited to be printed, which none of them could get hindered, seeing it has been many times reprinted in Germany, and is extant in all the famous libraries in Europe.†

* Cardinal Beaton, on account of his opposition to the English treaty, was imprisoned at Seton by the Estates. According to John Knox (History, i., 97; Edinb., 1846), he was liberated through bribes given to Maitland and Lord Seton. The cardinal's release forms the subject of a letter of Sir Ralph Sadler. No blame is imputed to Maitland. (Sir R. Sadler's State Papers, i., p. 136. Edinb., 1809, 4to.)

† George Buchanan was born at Killearn, Stirlingshire, in February, 1506. Having studied the classics in Paris, and philosophy at St. Andrews, he imbibed the doctrines of Luther, and became a keen supporter of the Reformation. His poem on the Franciscan Friars appeared in 1538; he was in the following year subjected to imprisonment by Cardinal Beaton, but effected his escape. He became Professor of Latin at Bourdeaux; he subsequently proceeded to Portugal, where he officiated as a professor in the University of Coimbra. As an upholder

3. Sir Richard Cockburn, of Clerkington, by the moyen of his grandfather, Sir Richard Maitland, was made Keeper of the Privy Seal, which place he enjoyed above thirty years, till he died, with all the remanent privileges that his grandfather had, viz., a lord of council, session, and exchequer. But these never augmented his estate in any sort, nor conquest he either land or heritage whatsoever. Only he left one son, now laird of Clerkington; what success he shall have will be known in process of time.*

4. Thomas, Earl of Haddington, after he had been the King's Advocate and Clerk Register, was made Privy Seal, in imitation of the English; for thereby he got precedency of all the nobility. But he liked better to be secretary, being the more profitable place. Of his success therein was written before.†

5. Robert, Earl of Roxburgh,‡ had the place of Privy Seal

---

of the Protestant doctrines, he was thrown into the dungeons of the Inquisition, where he remained eighteen months. After some changes he returned to Scotland in 1560, when he became classical tutor to Queen Mary. In 1566 he was appointed Principal of St. Leonard's College, St. Andrews, and in the following year was, though a layman, elected Moderator of the General Assembly. In 1570 he was appointed preceptor to the young king, and was nominated Director of the Chancery. Some time afterwards he was chosen Lord Privy Seal, with a seat in Parliament. His great work, the History of Scotland, occupied the last twelve years of his life; it was completed only within a month of his decease. He died at Edinburgh on the 28th September, 1582, at the age of seventy-six. Sir John Scot's relation as to his being summoned before the council to answer for some passages in his History, is unsupported by contemporary evidence. In May, 1584, an Act of Parliament was passed finding that his History and treatise *de jure regni* contained certain passages which ought to be deleted. There was no other interference with the publication of his works. After Buchanan, Walter, Commendator of Blantyre, was Privy Seal, from 1513 till February, 1595, when he demitted. To him succeeded Sir Richard Cockburn, who died in 1626.

* Sir Richard Cockburn was son of Sir John Cockburn, and his wife Helen, daughter of Sir Richard Maitland of Lethington. He was appointed Secretary of State in April, 1591, and in November of the same year was admitted a Lord of Session. When the Octavians obtained power he was forced to exchange with John Lindsay, of Balcarres, his post of secretary for that of Lord Privy Seal. He died in 1626.—*Anderson's Scottish Nation.*

† See *supra.*

‡ Sir Robert Ker, created Earl of Roxburgh 18th September, 1616, was born about 1570. He was one of twelve gentlemen knighted at the coronation of Queen Anne of Denmark in 1590. He accompanied James VI. to London in 1603. He was chosen one of the Lords of the Articles in the parliament of 1621; in the

bestowed upon him in his old age, albeit his first journey on horseback, in the year 1585, was at the raid of Stirling; at which time he had on a jack, being about fifteen years of age: thither he went, with others of the nobility, to rescue the king out of the hands of these courtiers, who then had his ear.

His family rose, from the style of Andrew Ker of Altounburne in King James III.'s time, to be lairds of Cessford, for their good services done at the siege of Roxburgh. And he himself was made Earl by King James VI. after his going to England.

He had a son of great expectation with his first wife, Lethington's daughter, who died in ———, and another son, begotten of Lady Jean Drummond, called Harie Lord Ker, who being married, by the unruly government of his youth shortly died without heirs male: so that the father behoved to tailzie the estate to another family; and pretermitting the house of Newbottle, who was really the nearest of blood to him, for causes known to himself, he made choice of his grandson by his daughter, third son to the Earl of Perth, whom he appointed to marry the eldest daughter of his son, and to assume the name of Ker. He had no learning, albeit all writs directed to him, as Lord Privy Seal, are in Latin. He was thrust out of the place divers years * before his death, and declared an enemy to the country by Act of Parliament.

Clerks of Register.

1. Thomas Marjoribanks,† of Ratho, was Clerk Register in 1553,

---

same parliament he voted for the confirmation of the Five Articles of Perth. In 1637 he was appointed Lord Privy Seal; he was deprived of that office by the Estates in 1649, consequent on his supporting the ill-fated "engagement" of the preceding year. He died on the 18th January, 1650, in his eightieth year. Lord Roxburgh was thrice married. By his first wife, a daughter of Sir William Maitland of Lethington, he had a son, Lord William Ker, who died in 1618, and three daughters. By his second wife, a daughter of the third Lord Drummond, he had one son, styled Lord Ker after his brother's death; he also predeceased his father. Lord Roxburgh married, thirdly, Lady Isobel Douglas, fifth daughter of the second Earl of Morton, without issue.

* Not "divers years;" just eleven months elapsed between Lord Roxburgh's deprivation of office in February, 1649, and his death in January, 1650.

† On the institution of the Court of Session in 1532, Thomas Marjoribanks was one of ten advocates selected to plead before the Lords. Conjointly with Dr. Gladstanes, he was appointed Advocate for the Poor in March, 1535. He acquired the

and that land, and what he then acquired lasted no longer than the third generation; for his grandson John sold all to the queen's tailor, Mr. Duncan, some twenty years ago.

2. Mr. James Balfour, thereafter Sir James,* succeeded in the place of Mr. James Scot, Dictator of the Rolls, and one of the Clerks of Session in *anno* 1560.

He first professed himself to be for religion; but, as Knox says fol. 82, he quitted the same, and said it was no marvel, being come of the house of Monquhannie; for in them, he says, was neither fear of God, nor love of virtue, farther than the present commodity persuaded them.

He was one of those that were taken by the French galleys out of the castle of St. Andrews after the slaughter of the cardinal, and was carried prisoner to France, and returned to Scotland out of

---

lands of Ratho in September, 1540. In the same year he was chosen Lord Provost of Edinburgh, and commissioner from the city to the Estates. He was admitted a Lord of Session, and appointed Clerk Register in February, 1549; he was deprived of the latter office in 1554, on the charge of having falsified a warrant. —*Anderson's Scottish Nation.*

* This celebrated Clerk Register was son of Sir Michael Balfour of Mountquhannie, Fifeshire. His brother David was one of the assassins of Cardinal Beaton; he joined the conspirators in the castle of St. Andrews, and on its surrender in June, 1547, was carried to France in the same galley with John Knox. On his return to Scotland in 1549 he abandoned his former friends, and is believed to have returned to the Romish faith. His perversity is severely censured by Knox. Among those who publicly embraced the Protestant doctrines in the castle of St. Andrews, the Reformer writes, "was he that now eyther rewillis, or ellis misrewillis Scotland, to wit, Schir James Balfour, (sometimes called Maister James), the cheaf and principall Protestant that there was to be found in this realme. This we wryte, becaus we have heard that the said Maister James alledgeis that he was never of this our religioun, but that he was brought up in Martine's (Luther's) opinioun of the sacrament, and tharefoir he can nott communicat with us. But his awin conscience and two hundreth witness besyde, know that he lyes; and that he was one of the cheaff (yf he had not been after Coppis) that wold have given his lyef, yf men mycht credite his wordis, for defence of the doctrin that the said Johnne Knox tawght. But albeit that those that never war of us (as none of Monquhanye's sones have schawin thame sellis to be) departe from us, it is no great wonder; for it is propir and naturall that the children follow the father; and lest the godly levar of that rase and progeny be schawin for yf in thame be eather fear of God, or luif of vertew, farther then the present commoditie persuades thame, men of judgement ar deceaved." (Knox's History, Edinb., 1846, 8vo., vol. i., p. 202.)

France in 1550. He calls him blasphemous Balfour, now called Clerk Register, in 1566.

In 1559, the said Mr. James sent his boy with a letter out of Leith, to advertise the queen's party of all that the congregation did; and is tainted likeways by Buchanan for revealing to those of the congregation, the sending out of the castle of Edinburgh the queen's silver box to the Earl of Bothwell, and to have advertised those of the king's faction to apprehend it; wherein were all the secrets of the queen's marriage, and love-letters to Bothwell.

He also it was who was the death of the Earl of Morton, and produced the contract wherein it was resolved to kill the king.* And being captain of the castle of Edinburgh, by the means of Sir Robert Melvill, he agreed with Morton to surrender the same to him, and got for the doing thereof the lands of Strathkinness and Ballone, which his successors brook to this day only by that title.

He was first styled parson of Flisk, then Prior of Pittenweem, being one of the lords of the spiritual side.

How he attained to be Laird of Burleigh, whether by marriage or conquest, I am not yet informed; † but it is sure Sir Michael Balfour, his son, having but one daughter, behoved, for the great

---

* In 1559 Balfour gave active support to the Queen Regent against the Lords of the Congregation. About 1560 he was appointed parson of Flisk. In November, 1561, he was nominated an Extraordinary Lord of Session by the title of Lord Pittendriech; in 1563 he was appointed an ordinary lord. He was sworn of the Privy Council in July, 1565. On the night of Rizzio's murder he was with Queen Mary at Holyrood; he was knighted by the queen on the 25th March, 1566, and appointed Clerk Register. He was a main instrument in accomplishing the death of Lord Darnley. In 1567 he was appointed Deputy Keeper of Edinburgh Castle and Lord President of the Court of Session. The story of his conspiring to allow the silver casket containing Queen Mary's letters to fall into the hands of the confederated lords is related by Buchanan (Hist., L. xviii., p. 51). On Queen Mary's imprisonment he attached himself to the Regent Murray, and was present at Langside in opposition to his benefactress. (Melvill's Memoirs, p. 202.) On the assassination of the Regent Lennox in 1570, he returned to the queen's party; in 1572 he made his peace with the Regent Morton, but joined the enemies of that nobleman in 1578. At Morton's trial he produced the celebrated bond, subscribed by him and others, for the support of Bothwell after Darnley's murder. Balfour died about 1584. He is the supposed author of the collection of Decisions known as "Balfour's Practicks."

† Sir James Balfour married Margaret, only child and heiress of Michael Balfour, of Burleigh, county of Kinross.

burden of debt he was in, to contract her with Robert Arnot's eldest son, who was depute-comptroller; who undertook to pay the whole burdens of the house, and quitted the name of Arnot, and took on him the name of Balfour; and yet the first year of their marriage there was evil agreement. Her son of that marriage, at his return from France, without the father's consent, took to wife at London the daughter of Sir William Balfour, of Pitcullo, sometime captain of the Tower of London; whereat the father was so incensed, that he did what in him lay to get the marriage dissolved by the General Assembly, in respect there was no copulation, because the young man had a wound open on him, which he had got in France some time before the marriage. Yet, within a year thereafter, the young folks agreed and came together, who as yet had no favourable countenance of the father; whether he shall again accept them in kindness is not known. But he has married one of his daughters to his brother's son, of intention, as many think, to dispone his estate to them in prejudice of his said son.

3. Mr. James Macgill, of Rankeillor-nether,* was a man of good learning. He accompanied the Earl of Murray in sundry embassies to England, and has very good commendations, by all the writers, of his honesty and fidelity in all his employments; yet has his son disponed the best barony of land that he conquest, viz., Pinkie, four miles from Edinburgh, which he sold thirty years ago to the Earl of Dunfermline, and contents himself with the lands of Old Lindores and Rankeillor in Fife.

After his decease, King James could hardly find a fit person to make clerk-register, in respect that Robert Scot,† eldest clerk of session, to whom the place by right was due, refused the same,

* Descended from a Galloway family of the name, Sir James Makgill purchased the estate of Nether Rankeillor, Fifeshire, and of Pinkie, near Edinburgh. Educated for the law, he was appointed Clerk Register in June, 1554. During the same year he was admitted a Lord of Session by the judicial title of Lord Rankeillor. He was sworn a member of the Privy Council in 1561. Being implicated in the murder of Rizzio, he was deprived of his Clerk-Registership in 1566; but the office was through favour of the Regent Murray restored to him in the following year. In 1568 he attended the regent at York to conduct the accusation against Queen Mary; he was an ambassador at the court of Elizabeth in 1571 and 1572. In 1578 he and George Buchanan were chosen extraordinary members of the Privy Council. He died in 1579. Sir James Makgill was an esteemed friend of John Knox.

† See Memoir of Sir John Scot, at the commencement of this volume.

telling his Majesty "that upon no terms he would be a lord:" whereupon, by the Earl of Mar's moyen, Alexander Hay, * clerk of the Council, was preferred; and because the said Robert Scot voluntarily consented to his admission, the said Alexander Hay resigned his place of Director of the Chancellery in 1577; which place the said Robert and his successors have enjoyed, by his son and grandson, till the year 1651. This Alexander Hay died clerk-register, but conquest little or no land; but a fair house in Edinburgh, which was sold to Mr. John Dawling by his son Sir Alexander Hay.

4. Sir John Skene † succeeded to be clerk-register after Alexander Hay; and was preferred to the place by the moyen of my Lord Blantyre, his brother-in-law; for their wives were two sisters.

He was well skilled in the laws before he was advanced to that place, and got a sole gift for printing the Acts of Parliament and *Regiam majestatem;* by which means he acquired a great deal of money from the country; for all heritors of lands were obliged to buy them: but it did little good; for albeit he lived many years in the place, yet did he purchase but few lands, only he bought Currie Hill and Ravelrig, of no great value; all which were sold by his son Sir James.

He resigned his place to his said son in his old age: but Haddington, by his power, forced his son Sir James to resign the same in his favour, and got him made an ordinary Lord of the Session, which place Sir James brooked till his death, and was made President of the Session by King Charles. But being of a generous

* Alexander Hay, descended from the old family of Hay, of Park, became Clerk of the Privy Council in March, 1564. He was afterwards appointed Director of the Chancery, an office which he resigned in 1577 for that of Clerk Register. In the same year he was made an Ordinary Lord of Session, and assumed the judicial title of Lord Easter Kennet. In 1589 he attended James VI. to Denmark as interim Secretary of State. He died 19th September, 1594.

† Sir John Skene was born in 1549; he studied at the Universities of Aberdeen and St. Andrews, and afterwards travelled in Denmark, Norway, and Sweden. Studying law, he passed advocate in March, 1575. He accompanied James VI. to Norway in 1589, and in 1591 was sent as ambassador to the States-General. In 1594 he was appointed Clerk Register, and in the same year was admitted an ordinary Lord of Session, when he assumed the judicial title of Lord Currichill. In 1596 he was appointed one of the Octavians, or eight Commissioners of Exchequer. He was commissioned to edit and print the laws of the realm, which he satisfactorily accomplished. He died in March, 1612.

disposition, and having small means, he behoved to sell and dispone all, both in town and country, for defraying of his debts.

Sir John's four daughters had little better success; only Sir William Scot's wife, who got nothing by her father, had best success. But the other three, one of them married to Robert Learmont, advocate, the second to my Lord Fosterseat, and the third to Sir Robert Richardson of Pentcaitland, their sons have disponed all their father's lands, and nothing is left thereof at this day.

5. Sir Alexander Hay attained to his father's place of Clerk-register,* but was not learned, neither came he ever to any estate of lands.

One remarkable thing he did, viz., having found amongst his father's writs a bond of Sir William Scott, uncle to Sir John Scot, Director of the Chancellary, whereby he obliged himself, at Sir John's attaining to the age of twenty-one years, to resign the office of Director of the Chancellary and Clerkship in his favour, which he had brooked as tutor during all the said Sir John's minority; but, instead of delivering the same to Sir John, as was designed to have been given him by his grandfather, he gave it to Mr. Robert Williamson, who was the said Sir William Scott's servant, and he put it in the fire that it might never come to light: but God, the protector of orphans, revenged the injury in a strange way; for the said Mr. Robert, in his sister's house, Archibald Law's wife, being sickly, and left alone, fell in the fire in an apoplexy, and burnt his head and hands before any came near him. This bond was written by Adam Lawtie, writer, and subscribed by Sir William, Adam Cowpar, Clerk to the Bills, and Mr. Robert Williamson, witnesses, and was given by umquhile Robert Scot in keeping to the said Sir Alexander's father.

Sir Alexander, his son, brooks a piece of land he got of his uncle, called Monkton. His daughter was married to the Laird of Kilspindie, who, finding her barren, took other women, and she got a divorcement of him for that cause.

6. Sir John Hamilton,† brother to the Earl of Haddington, was

---

* The Earl of Haddington succeeded Sir John Skene in May, 1612, but demitted in October following, when he was appointed Secretary of State. Sir Alexander Hay received the office of Register 30th July, 1612. He was previously a Lord of Session, by the title of Lord Newton.

† Sir George Hay, afterwards Lord High Chancellor, was admitted Clerk

preferred to that place of clerk-register by the credit of the Marquis of Hamilton and his brother.

He was a good man, but void of learning; and never conquest anything to his posterity. He had no heirs-male; and of what his daughters had, I think little or nothing is left to their posterity; and his lands, called Magdalen's, are also disponed since his decease to one Dundas.

7. Sir John Hay* was Town-clerk of Edinburgh, and was advanced by the king and queen when the Bishop of St. Andrews was in credit with his Majesty. He was also made provost of Edinburgh, and undertook stoutly to cause the ministers of Edinburgh accept of the Service Book in the churches there. But there being a mutiny in the town, and the bishops chased down the streets for attempting that rash enterprise, he was forced to quit the town, and fly to England, where he joined himself to James Graham, and, at the battle of Philiphaugh, was taken prisoner, and likely to have suffered death, if he had not been freed by the means of the Earl of Callander, whose lady was his kinswoman, and of his son, Mr. William, who advanced £500 sterl. to some of the officers for his relief. He has lurked ever since privately, and never conquest any lands, but a poor piece in Galloway, called the Land.

8. Sir Alexander Gibson, of Durie, † having been long a Clerk of

---

Register 26th March, 1616; he was succeeded by Sir John Hamilton 27th July, 1622, who was also admitted an ordinary Lord of Session under the title of Lord Magdalens. He was deprived of his Judgeship in 1626, consequent on a resolution of Charles II. that no officer of state should sit in the Court of Session. On the 2nd November, 1630, he was admitted an extraordinary Lord of Session. (Brunton and Haig, 269.) He died at Holyrood House, 28th November, 1632.

* Sir John Hay was descended from a younger brother of Sir David Hay, of Yester, ancestor of the noble family of Tweeddale. He delivered a Latin address to James VI. on his visit to Edinburgh in 1617, which is preserved in the "Muses' Welcome." He was knighted by Charles I. in March, 1632, and in the following January was nominated Clerk Register and a Lord of Session. He strongly urged the introduction of the Service Book in 1637, and was in consequence obliged to seek personal safety in England. Returning to Scotland, he was accused of treason and imprisoned in Edinburgh Castle. Captured on the field of Philiphaugh, he escaped the scaffold by having, as was believed, bribed the Earl of Lanark with the rents of his estate. He died on the 20th November, 1654.

† Sir Alexander Gibson was appointed one of the Clerks of Session, 25th July, 1632; he was nominated Clerk Register 13th November, 1641. He resisted the

Session, was made Clerk-Register when the king came last to Scotland, by the moyen of William Murray, now Earl of Dysart; to whom it is said he gave a velvet cassock, lined with fine furrings, and a thousand double pieces therein.

He was very well skilled to be a judge; but, within a few years, having gone to England to the engagement with the Marquis of Hamilton, he was thrust from the place, and has lived since that time a private man.

9. Sir Archibald Johnston was both Advocate and Clerk-Register successively;* yet here he is insert in this short catalogue by the

---

introduction of the Service Book in 1638, and was much opposed to the bishops. As Clerk of Parliament he refused to read the royal warrant proroguing Parliament in November, 1639. In the following year he was appointed Commissary-General of the forces raised against the king. He was admitted a Lord of Session 2nd July, 1646, but having joined "the engagement" he was deprived by the Act of Classes in 1649. In August, 1652, he was elected one of the Scottish Commissioners to attend the Parliament of England. He died in June, 1656. Sir Alexander was eldest son of Sir Alexander Gibson, Baronet, Lord Durie, an eminent lawyer, and author of "Durie's Practicks," a valuable collection of Decisions in Scottish Law. ("Balfour's Annals," II., 276, 293, 298.—Brunton and Haig, 317.)

* Sir Archibald Johnston was son of James Johnston, of Beirholm, Dumfriesshire, formerly a merchant in Edinburgh, by his wife, Elizabeth, daughter of the celebrated Sir Thomas Craig. He passed advocate in 1633. Having zealously attached himself to the Presbyterian cause, he prepared jointly with the Earl of Rothes the supplication against innovations presented to the Privy Council in September, 1637. Along with Alexander Henderson he revised the Covenant, which was renewed in March, 1638. He was chosen clerk to the famous General Assembly which met at Glasgow in that year. He was one of the commissioners who negotiated the treaty of Berwick. By Charles I. in 1641 he was knighted and appointed an ordinary Lord of Session, with a pension of £200 a year. He represented the county of Edinburgh in the Estates of Parliament in 1643, and in the following year was chosen a commissioner to attend the English Parliament, and the Assembly of Divines at Westminster. In 1646 he was appointed Lord Advocate; in that capacity he proclaimed Charles II. as King in February, 1649. In March of the same year he succeeded Sir Alexander Gibson as Clerk Register. Subsequent to the battle of Dunbar in 1650 he lived in retirement till 1657, when being persuaded to go to London, he received from Cromwell restoration to his office of Clerk Register, and was by the Protector created Lord Warriston, and appointed a commissioner for the Administration of Justice in Scotland. At the Restoration an order was issued for his apprehension, but having received timely notice he escaped to Hamburgh. He was outlawed 10th October, 1661, and a reward offered for his apprehension. In 1662 he proceeded to Rouen, in France, for the sake of his health. He was there seized by authority of Charles I.,

style of Clerk of Register, being his last place, and most honourable in the state. For, as for that first of the king's advocate, he attained to it without craving it from the king; but having, for £1,000 sterl. got Sir Thomas Hope's demission, he was accepted in the place by the Parliament, which he did for helping on of his daughter's marriage; and finding himself weak in body, and not very acceptable to the Parliament, not remembering these lines of his grandfather, Mr. Thomas Craig, lib. 2 *de feudis*. *Qui ad honores juridicos pretio per veniunt, pretio etiam eos vendere oportet.*

When he came to be Clerk Register, albeit he possessed great sincerity in religion, and for that was in great credit, yet he admitted sundry to be Clerks of the Session under him, who before had been deprived by the Parliament for malignancy, such as Mr. William Hay and his cousin, Sir John Gibson, for sums of money given to his lady; and when his place was declared void at the incoming of the English, as all other offices were, fearing to be challenged for that by those whom he had wronged, he transacted of new again with them, and gave them a part of their money back again that they might be silent, and not complain. But in these five or six years wherein he was an officer, he conquest no lands but Warriston, of the avail of 1,000 merks *Scots* a year, where he now lives freed of trouble of state or country.

* He was the last Clerk Register, and a Lord of the Session; and being in England, was taken prisoner, and sent home to Scotland, and for the crimes contained in his dittay was publicly executed to death at Edinburgh at the market cross, *anno* 1663.

JUSTICE-CLERKS.

1. Mr. Richard Lawson, justice-clerk, conquest a good estate about Edinburgh, near the Burrow-loch, and the barony of Boighall, which his grandson, Sir William Lawson, of Boighall, dilapidated and sold; he went to Holland to the wars.

---

and being brought to London was consigned to the Tower. He was afterwards sent to Edinburgh, and was condemned to death by the Parliament. He was hanged at the Cross of Edinburgh on the 22nd July, 1663. On the scaffold he conducted himself with entire self-possession.

* This paragraph appears, from the close of the last, to have been added by the author some years afterwards. — *Goodal.*

2. Thomas, Sir John, and Sir Lewis Ballantyne, grandfather, father, and son, were all successively, after others, justice-clerks;* but Sir John made the conquests, and left to his eldest son, Sir Lewis, a fair estate, viz., the barony of Broughton, with the superiority of the Canongate, and North-leith, having therein near two thousand vassals; the baronies of Achnoul, Woodhouslie, Abbot's Grange, and many others. And to the eldest son of the third marriage he left the barony of Carlowrie, and Kilconquhar in Fife, and divers lands about Brechin.

Sir Lewis was a Lord of the Session, Council, and Exchequer; but, by curiosity, he dealt with a warlock, called Richard Graham,† to raise the devil, who having raised him in his own yard in the Canongate, he was thereby so terrified, that he took sickness and thereof died. And having left his lady, sister to the Lord Livingston, a great conjunct-fee, the Earl of Orkney married her, and, after some years, having moved her to sell her conjunct-fee lands, and having disposed of all the moneys of the same, sent her back to the Canongate, where she lived divers years very miserably, and there died in extreme poverty.

* Thomas Bannatyne, or Bellenden, of Auchinoul, was in June, 1535, appointed an Ordinary Judge in the Court of Session. In 1538 he was nominated Director of Chancery, and in 1539 was raised to the office of Justice-Clerk. He died in 1546. On the 20th June, 1547, the elder of his two sons, Sir John Bellenden of Auchinoul, was appointed Justice-Clerk, and about the same time an Ordinary Lord of Session. By Mary of Guise Sir John was appointed to act as mediator between her and the lords of the congregation; he afterwards attached himself to the latter. He was sworn of the Privy Council in 1561. He was implicated in the murder of Rizzio, but becoming reconciled to the queen, he gave countenance to her union with Bothwell. He afterwards joined the association against the queen, and became a counsellor and friend of the Regent Murray. Indirectly he was the cause of the Regent's death by procuring a pardon for Hamilton of Bothwellhaugh for some crime which endangered his life. In 1573 he took part in arranging the pacification of Perth. He died in 1577. By Sir Lewis Bellenden, his eldest son, he was succeeded in the office of Justice-Clerk. Sir Lewis was concerned in the Raid of Ruthven, but escaped punishment. In 1584 he was appointed an Ordinary Lord of Session. He had a principal share in the downfall of Arran in 1585, and accompanied James VI. on his matrimonial expedition to Norway in 1589. He died in August, 1591. (Brunton and Haig, 57, 91, 194.)

† Richard Graham, the wizard, was one of those with whom the Earl of Bothwell was accused of consulting in regard to the life of the king. (Melvill's Memoirs, 353.)

Sir Lewis's eldest son, Sir James, sold the haill lands to his uncle, the Earl of Roxburgh, and he to the town of Edinburgh.

The other brother, the laird of Kilconquhar, sporting himself on the loch in a boat, was there drowned; and his only son dying young, Mr. Adam, his uncle, succeeded to the land, who was Bishop of Dunblane, and sold the same lands to Sir John Carstairs, being a little before expelled the kingdom with the rest of the bishops, by Act of Parliament.

3. Sir John Cockburn, of Ormiston, attained next to that place,* having married Sir Lewis's half-sister, the goodwife of Humbie, whose only son of her first marriage, Sir James Lawson, running his horse at full speed on the sands near Aberdeen, sunk, horse and all, and was never seen again.

His two sons, Mr. John and James Cockburn, were greatly subject to drunkenness and companionry. His grandson died young, but sold the barony of Paistoun, and a number of lands about Lammermuir, called the Hairhead; and left only the lands of Ormiston to his son, greatly engaged, who was in a way to have recovered that broken estate by the help of his father-in-law, Sir Adam Hepburn, of Humbie, if they had not been both taken prisoners by the English at Elicht, and carried to London in 1651.

4. Sir George Elphinston, of Blythswood, justice-clerk, was in his youth in great credit with King James VI., and lay in bed with him many years; but was discourted by the means of Sir George Home, before the King's going to England. Thereafter he lived a private life in his old age; at which time King Charles made him justice-clerk, which he brooked till his dying day,† but had as little good luck as the rest; for his burden of debts was so great that his son's tutors behoved to sell the lands immediately after his death, which were worth 10,000 merks per annum. He left only one son behind him, who had two thumbs on each hand.

5. Sir John Hamilton, of Orbiston, succeeded him in that place: ‡

---

* Sir John Cockburn, of Ormiston, was admitted an Extraordinary Lord of Session 4th July, 1588, and was appointed Justice-Clerk in 1591. He was one of the commissioners who proceeded to England, in 1604, to treat of the union, then projected. He died in June, 1623. ("Balfour's Annals," II., 97. Brunton and Haig, 217.)

† He was Justice Clerk from 1625 till 1633.

‡ Sir James Carmichael succeeded to Sir George Elphinston in 1634, and in

he conquest the barony of Areskine; but being a malignant, and a follower of his chief, the Duke of Hamilton, he lost thereby all his places, by Act of Parliament in 1648.

King's Advocates.

1. Mr. Robert Crichton, advocate,* left a fair estate behind him, viz., the barony of Eliok and Cluny, to his son Sir Robert Crichton, of Cluny. But after he had killed the laird of Moncoffer, in revenge of the Earl of Murray's slaughter, at the chapel of Eglismaly, he had never good success in his affairs.

His eldest brother James,† as Manutius says, was a miracle of nature, seeing he could forget nothing; but he was killed by the young Duke of Mantua, whom he attended, coming out from the duke's mistress; and by that means Sir Robert fell to be laird, but has sold all the lands in his own time, and at this day no memory is left of them.

He was descended, as all thereafter of that name were, from the house of the Lord Crichton, who was Chancellor in King James II.'s

---

1637 was made Treasurer Depute; and Sir John Hamilton succeeded to Carmichael.—*Goodal.*

* Robert Crichton, of Eliock, was appointed Lord Advocate, conjointly with John Spens, of Condie, in February, 1560. After the death of the Regent Murray, Queen Mary requested Crichton to visit her in England, but he was kept from going by the Regent Lennox. In 1581 he was raised to the Bench. He died in June, 1582.

† James Crichton, styled "the Admirable," was son of Robert Crichton, Lord Advocate. He was born about 1557, and studied at St. Andrews. Before attaining his twentieth year he is said to have mastered the circle of the sciences, and to have understood ten languages. He excelled in all personal accomplishments. Proceeding to Paris he challenged the Professors of the University and other learned persons to dispute with him, and acquitted himself to admiration. At Rome he astonished and delighted the Pope in a public disputation; he afterwards publicly disputed at Venice and Padua. At Mantua he proved his dexterity by overcoming and slaying a noted and dangerous prize-fighter. By the Duke of Mantua he was appointed tutor to his son, a youth of licentious manners. One night during the Carnival of 1582, or 1583, as he was rambling about the streets, playing on his guitar, he was attacked by six persons in masks. He dispersed his assailants and disarmed their leader, whom he discovered to be the prince, his pupil. Stooping down, he handed to the prince his sword, who took it, and plunged it into his heart. A memoir of the Admirable Crichton was published in 1823 by Patrick Fraser Tytler.

time, and was forfeited for holding out his house against the king's authority;* and lately all the cadets of him are decayed, and have little or no lands left undisposed: for the Lord Sanquhar, in 1612, having caused his footman to kill a fencer who had thrust out his eye at fencing, he was thereafter hanged at London; and his estate, by King James VI.'s decree-arbitral, was taken from his bastard son, to whom it was tailzied, and given to his cousin William, of Rye-hill, who was thereafter made Earl of Dumfries, and lived divers years at Doncaster with the Lady Swift, whom he married after her husband's decease. But he sold all the estate before his death to the Earl of Kinnoul and Lord Queensberry.

The next family was the Viscount of Frendraught, who decayed after killing the laird of Rothiemay, and the burning of his own tower (committed, as *fama clamosa* said, by his own lady), wherein the Lord Aboyne and other four were burnt quick.†

All the rest of the barons of the surname of Crichton, viz., Cairns, Cranston-riddel, Innernytie, Lugton, Waughton, Strathurd, Abercrombie, Brunstone, and Arbickie, have had no better success; but their lands are all in the hands of strangers, by alienation of them in their own time.

2. Mr. John Spence, of Condie, advocate,‡ having conquest the

* This was not the Chancellor's own house, but the Castle of Edinburgh; the occasion of which was this: He had decoyed William, Earl of Douglas, David, his brother, and Sir Malcolm Fleming, of Cumbernauld, into the castle, and there murdered them in 1441. The Chancellor, fearing the resentment of William, Earl of Douglas, cousin to the last Earl William, who soon after got into the king's favour, retired to the Castle of Edinburgh. Douglas caused summon him to answer the charge of treason and breach of trust, and in absence he was declared rebel, and his estate forfeited. He himself was besieged in the castle, which he held out for nine months, but at length surrendered it, and was pardoned. He was soon received again into favour, and a second time made Chancellor.—*Goodal.*

† See *supra.*

‡ Sir John Spence was Lord Advocate in 1563, when John Knox was brought by Queen Mary before her Privy Council, on the charge of sedition. Being favourable to the Reformers and the Protestant cause, Spence waited upon Knox in private, to ascertain the nature of his defence. Having listened to the Reformer, Spence said, "I thank God I came to you with a fearfull and sorrowfull heart, fearing yee had committed some offence punishable by the lawes, which would have brought no small griefe to the hearts of all those who have receaved the Word of Life out of your mouth. But I depart greatlie rejoicing, als weill becaus I perceave yee have comfort in the middest of your troubles, as

baronies of Gilmerton in Lothian, Kilmux and Condie in Fife, had only three daughters: one of them was married to Herring of Lethinty, whose son Sir David sold all his lands of Lethinty, Gilmerton, and Glasclune, in his own time. Another was married to James Ballantyne, of Spout, whose son James took the same course; the third to Sir John Moncrieff, by whom he had an only son, who after his marriage went mad, and leapt into the river of Earn, and there perished; but left a son of good expectation, who had no land by his grandfather.

3. Mr. David Borthwick, King's Advocate,* conquest many lands in Lothian and Fife, as Balnacrieff, Admiston, Balcarras, and others; but having insest his son Sir James therein in his own time, he never rested till he had sold all. And it being told the father, who was lying on his death-bed, that he had lately sold Balnacrieff, the old man is said to have spoken these words,—"What shall I say? I give him to the devil that gets a fool, and makes not a fool of him." With which words he expired. These words are kept to this day as a byword, and called " Mr. David Borthwick's Testament."

4. Mr. David Macgill, King's Advocate,† conquest a great estate, as the baronies of Cranston, Nisbets, &c., which as yet his grandson Sir James enjoys.

But Sir James's eldest son, notwithstanding all the pains taken on him in his education, quitted the kingdom, and took himself to be a single soldier some ten years ago; and no man that knows the father thinks him so simple as to leave his estate to such an heir.

---

that I cleerelie understand yee have not committed suche a crime as is bruited, yee will be accused; but God will assist you." At the Council, Spence accused the Reformer "verie gentlie," and he was at once acquitted. ("Calderwood's History," Edinb., 1843, Vol. II., p. 234, 237.)

* Mr. David Borthwick was one of nine procurators selected by the Court of Session, in March, 1549, to plead "before thame in all actions and causes." He was, in 1552, member of a commission appointed to treat with English commissioners upon Border affairs. He was employed as counsel by the Corporations of Aberdeen and Edinburgh. On the 12th May, 1567, as counsel for the Earl of Bothwell he took instruments of Queen Mary's pardon of him for her abduction. He became joint King's Advocate in 1573, and was the first who was styled Lord Advocate. He died in January, 1581. (Acts of Sederunt, 1811—48. Brunton and Haig, 154.)

† In 1582. He died in 1596.

5. Sir William Oliphant, of Newton, advocate,* conquest the lands of Newton, the barony of Strabroke, and the Murrows near Edinburgh; but was as unfortunate in his children as any of the rest; for his eldest son, Sir James, after he was honoured to be a lord of session, was expelled therefrom for having shot his own gardener dead with a hackbut. His eldest son, viz., Sir James, procreate on Inchbraikie's daughter, in his drunken humours, stabbed his mother with a sword in her own house, and for that fled to Ireland. He disponed and sold the whole lands, and died in great penury.

The second brother, Mr. William, lay many years in prison, and disponed that barony of Strabroke and Kirkhill to Sir Lewis Stewart, who at this day enjoys the same.

6. Sir Thomas Hope † was created advocate after the death of Sir William Oliphant, who possessed the said place both in the time of King James and King Charles.

He conquest the baronies of Craighall, Grantoun, and Greenlaw, wherein he caused his son Sir John infeft his grandson, who at this time is a minor.

He assisted and gave counsel to the Earl of Menteith, and concurred with him in his service as heir to King Robert II.‡ His

* Mr. John Skene was King's Advocate in 1589; Mr. William Hart, of Livelands, in 1594. Mr. Thomas Hamilton, afterwards Earl of Haddington, was conjoined with Mr. Macgill in 1595, and was after his death sole advocate till 1612, when Sir William Oliphant succeeded, who kept it till 1626.—*Goodal.*

† Sir Thomas Hope was son of an eminent merchant, and passed advocate at an early age. He distinguished himself at the trial of the six ministers, who, in 1606, were arraigned at Linlithgow on a charge of high treason, because they had in ecclesiastical matters resisted royal authority. In 1626 he was appointed Lord Advocate; he was created a baronet in 1628. In 1638 he took part in framing the National Covenant, and he supported the legality of the famous General Assembly of that year. By Charles I. he was appointed Lord High Commissioner to the General Assembly of 1643. He died in 1646.

‡ William, Earl of Menteith, was served heir to his ancestor, David, Earl of Strathern, and had a patent from K. Charles conferring that title upon him. But his vanity, supported by the error of our historians, that David, Earl of Strathern, was the eldest son of Robert II.'s first marriage with Eupham Ross, his queen, made him begin to drop some hints of his right to the crown; on which he was deprived of all his offices, and a reduction brought of his service. This gave occasion to Sir Lewis Stewart to confute that gross error in our historians, that his ancestor was a son of Robert II. by his first marriage; which he did by producing several authentic deeds by Robert II. himself: particularly one at the time of his coronation, declaring John Stuart, of Scotland, to be his true heir, and

eldest son thereupon being challenged by his Majesty, he behoved to come in his will; and after the said Earl of Menteith was degraded from all his honours, his Majesty took only a bond from the said Sir Thomas, acknowledging his fault, and obliging himself never to give his Majesty cause of offence thereafter; promising, if he did any fault, to suffer what that fault merited.

He advised a way to the lords of erection to get all the kirk-livings back again, contrary to an Act of Parliament whereby they were for ever annexed to the Crown, by causing them take a wadset of the same, and acknowledge in the writs that his Majesty was indebted in great sums of money, whereas indeed he was never owing any. This will not fail to be quarrelled by succeeding ages, and those who shall have authority, and apparently for that cause will be reduced.

He was barred with the rest of the officers of state from having a voice in Parliament, which the king's advocates had many years before, and had only licence to sit and speak, but no place to vote.*

In that year, when King Charles was last in Scotland, seeing himself in that case, and that all things were cross in the state, he transacted with Sir Archibald Johnston, and, upon certain conditions, best known to themselves, resigned the said place to him, and within a year or two died in Edinburgh.†

His son, Sir James, getting a part of his estate in West Lothian, therein found a lead ore mine, and having sold some of it to the Hollanders, the ship wherein it was perished with all that was in her.

---

to have the right to succeed after him to the kingdom; and another deed, or Act of Parliament, in the third year of his reign, by which he entailed the crown to his sons of both marriages, enumerating them all particularly by name. This was afterwards defended by the Earl of Cromarty, and was the subject of a very late dispute betwixt Mr. Logan and Mr. Thomas Ruddiman. But that controversy hath been since quite unravelled, and the ground of the mistake laid open, in a dissertation by Mr. John Gordon, Advocate, Professor of History in the College of Edinburgh.—*Goodal.*

* Before his time the King's Advocate used to plead uncovered; but he having two of his sons then upon the Bench, Sir John and Sir Thomas, the lords indulged him the privilege of pleading with his hat on, which his successors in office have ever since enjoyed.—*Goodal.*

† He was advocate from 1626 till 1641. To him succeeded Sir Archibald Johnston, and he being made Clerk Register in 1649, Sir Thomas Nicolson was made advocate, but continued short while.—*Goodal.*

COMPTROLLERS.

1. David Wood, of Craig, was comptroller,* and had a good estate, but his son dilapidated all, at least his grandson, and sold the same to the Lord Carnegie, one of whose sons is baron thereof.

2. Sir John Wishart, of Pitarrow,† was also comptroller in Queen Mary's time, but a great stickler in the time of the Reformation, as Knox mentions in his chronicle; but says he was a small friend to the ministers anent their stipends, and that he was more careful to make up his own house than to furnish them bread.

His son, Sir John Wishart, lived to a good age in good reputation, and was a principal baron of the Mearns, allied with Glenbervie, who became thereafter Earl of Angus.

But his sons had bad success; for Sir John, the eldest, contrary to his father's mind and express command, fell desperately in love with a daughter of the House of Carden, albeit his father endeavoured to the utmost of his power to hinder him, and gave him leave to marry any other woman in the world except her; but was loath to tell him the cause of his dissent; which was, that he had lyen with that woman's mother, and she was his own daughter. After which marriage all went backward among them. Sir John fled the country; his wife lived in England, and was maintained by the Lady Annandale, her cousin, having nothing of her own for many years.

The second brother, Mr. James, for debt, behoved to comprise the lands of Pitarrow, and stood infeft therein many years; but in the end, not being able to double out the debt, he involved himself in acquiring the same; he was forced not only to sell the lands of

---

* In the times of King James V. and of Queen Mary, viz., in 1538 and 1546. To him succeeded William, Commendator of Culross, in 1546 and 1553. Bartholomew Villemor, a Frenchman, had been named comptroller by Queen Mary in March, 1560-1, but they who had taken upon themselves the administration of affairs refused to admit him.—*Goodal.*

† John Wishart, Laird of Pitarrow, in Forfarshire, was son of Sir James Wishart, Justice-Clerk. In the Parliament of August, 1560, he was selected with a few others to administer state affairs. Some time after Queen Mary's arrival in Scotland he was appointed comptroller; he was succeeded by Sir William Murray, of Tullibardine, in 1564. He was one of the ten persons who were knighted on the occasion of the marriage of the Earl of Murray. He was appointed an Extraordinary Lord of Session 19th November, 1567; he accompanied the Regent Murray to England in 1568. He died 25th September, 1576. (Note by Mr. David Laing to Knox's History, vol. ii., 311.)

Monboddo, pertaining to himself, to Captain Irving, but even the barony of Pitarrow itself, to my Lord Carnegie, one of whose sons brooks the same to this day. He married Margaret Riccarton, and got a good portion with her; but being in necessity, they both behoved to go to Ireland, where he lived till the time of the late troubles; and in the beginning of them, being a captain, was killed in the field; and his wife, being in great necessity, returned to Edinburgh, where she has been maintained by the charity of her friends, having nothing of her own.

The third, Mr. William, was minister of Leith, but fled the country for refusing to subscribe the Covenant, and died some few years thereafter in Cornwall, leaving only one son, John, who was killed at Edgehill fighting in the king's service against the Parliament; and none knows what has become of his succession : so that the memory of that family is quite extinguished.*

3. Andrew Wood, of Largo, the descendant of that noble Wood of Largo† who, in King James IV.'s time, did so great vassalages at sea, and especially against an English sea-captain called Bull, with whom he grappled about the May, and having fought the English ships, was grounded at Dunbar Sands; and got the barony of Largo in heritage therefor. ‡

* Sir William Murray, of Tullibarden, succeeded to Pitarrow in 1563, and continued till 1581. Sir James Campbell, of Ardkinglas, was comptroller in 1584. —*Goodal.*

† The following note is on the margin of the oldest copy, but in later copies is engrossed into the texts :—" He had been first a skipper on the north side of the bridge of Leith, and being pursued, mortified his house to Paul's work, as the register bears."—*Goodal.*

‡ He had been a very faithful servant to King James III., and got from him the lands of Largo to keep his ship in trim, and afterwards got them in feu *anno* 1482, and was knighted by him. Mindful of the king's kindness, he remained constant in his affection to him, even after his death, and would not submit to the lords, whom he looked upon as traitors and murderers of the king. But he was afterwards prevailed upon to go and attack a fleet of five English ships of war, which infested the frith; and with his own two ships only, the *Flower* and the *Yellow Carvel*, he took them all and brought them up to Leith : and soon after K. Henry VII., to revenge the affront of this defeat, having equipped another fleet of three of his best men-of-war, commanded by Stephen Bull, who, on the promise of great rewards, undertook to bring Captain Wood to the king dead or alive, he, with the same two ships, fought that captain at the Isle of May, till the tide carried his ships to the mouth of Tay, where they stranded on the sandbanks; and there Captain Wood took the three English ships, and carried them up to Dundee.

He was comptroller in King James VI.'s time,* and went up with him to England, but had so evil success there, that he behoved to sell all his lands, and the same are now in the hands of Sir Alexander Gibson of Durie. The House of Lamielethem, a cadet of that family, who had a considerable estate in Fife, is also gone to decay, and the estates of the remanent families of that name are all lately sold to strangers, viz., Wood of Craig, sometime comptroller, and Wood of Grange; so that none of that name remain.

4. David Seton, of Parbroath, was comptroller in Queen Mary's time; † but his son disponed the whole lands, and they are now in the possession of the Earl of Crawford; so that the memory of that family is extinguished, albeit it was very numerous, and brave men descended thereof.

5. Sir George Home, of Wedderburn, was also comptroller to King James,‡ but had no better success than the rest of his predecessors; for he behoved to quit it, the king being much in his debt; which brought on such a burden on his house, that it is in hazard to perish, albeit there belonged to it a great patrimony. And the last two lairds, both father and son, were killed (being commanders at the unhappy field of Dunbar) by the English, as seven others of their forefathers had been before; so that never one of that house died in their beds, but only he who was comptroller.

6. Sir David Murray, of Gospertie, was thereafter comptroller, §

Our author therefore is mistaken, both as to the time of his getting the lands of Largo, and as to the place where he defeated Bull.—*Goodal.*

* From 1585 till 1587.

† It should be in K. James VI.'s time; for he was comptroller in 1589, and demitted in 1595.—*Goodal.*

‡ Sir George Home was appointed Warden of the East Marches in 1578, and Comptroller in 1597. He died 24th November, 1616. His only son, Sir David Home, of Wedderburn, along with his son George, fell at the battle of Dunbar in 1650.

§ Sir David Murray, of Gospertie, was a cadet of the noble family of Athole. He was appointed Comptroller in 1598, when he was also sworn of the Privy Council. He was at Perth with James VI. at the time of the Gowrie conspiracy, and afterwards obtained from the king the barony of Ruthven, which belonged to Gowrie. He accompanied the king to London in 1603, and was appointed a commissioner for the projected union of the kingdoms in 1605. He was created Lord Scone. As Lord High Commissioner to successive General Assemblies, he strove to introduce episcopacy. He was mainly instrumental in passing the Five Articles in the Assembly at Perth in 1618. On the ratification of the Articles by and rose to great grandeur, who before was master stabler; but being careful to augment the rents of the Crown, to the heavy prejudice of the king's tenants of the property of the barony of Auchtermuchtie, in Fife, the tenants were so exasperated thereat, that they invaded him; and one James Maxwell, having grappled with him, they both fell together to the ground. James being above him, cried to his son to strike through all, being willing to die himself that the comptroller might die also; and undoubtedly he had perished there, if the Laird of Balwearie had not intervened, and rescued him from the danger.

He was employed in great services by King James, and albeit an ignorant man, yet was he bold, and got great business effectuated; for he was the king's commissioner when the five articles concerning divine worship were brought in at Perth.

He left no succession behind him, but tailzied his estate, the half to the Laird of Balvaird, of whose house he was descended as a younger son, and the other half to the Earl of Annandale, who was his friend at court. Balvaird's part is yet entire, and the youth is hopeful; but as for Annandale's, his burdens are very great, and as yet has no succession.

7. James Hay, of Fingask, father to the Earl of Carlisle,* after

---

Parliament in 1621, he hastened to London to convey the intelligence to the king. For this act of service, and some others, he was raised in the peerage as Viscount Stormount. He died 27th August, 1631.

* James Hay, afterwards Earl of Carlisle, is thus described by Sir Anthony Weldon:—" The king no sooner came to *London* but notice was taken of a rising favourite, the first meteor of that nature appearing in our climate, as the king cast his eye upon him for affection, so did all the courtiers, to adore him. His name was Mr. *James Hay*, a gentleman that lived in *France*, and some say of the *Scottish* guard to that king. This gentleman coming over to meet the king, and share with him in his new conquest (according to the *Scottish* phrase), it should seem had some former acquaintance with the then Leiger Embassador in *Scotland* for the *French* king, who coming with his Majesty into *England*, presented this gentleman as a well-accomplished gentleman to the king in such an high commendation as engendered such a liking as produced a favourite; in thankful acknowledgment whereof, he did him many fair offices for the present, and coming afterwards an extraordinary embassador to our king, made him the most sumptuous feast at *Essex* House that ever was seen before, never equalled since, in which was such plenty, and fish of that immensity brought out of *Muscovia*, that dishes were made to contain them (no dishes in all *England* before could ne'er hold them), and after that a costly Voydee, and after that a Mask of choyse noble men and gentlemen, and after that a most costly and magnificent banquet, the king, lords, and all the

him was comptroller by the credit of his son, a great courtier with King James, who was the bringer in of Somerset to the court; and Somerset, to be rid of him at court, moved the king to employ him always in embassies abroad.

He married first the Lord Dennie's daughter, which lady, being in a coach at night in the streets of London, got her ear rent by a rogue, who pulled the diamond forth thereof, and with the fright she died. His next lady was Northumberland's daughter.

He was so lavish in expenses in his lifetime, that at his death he was addebted in vast sums of money, which never were paid to this day; so that his son behoved to quit England and go to the island of Barbadoes, which his father had got in gift from the king, where he lives till this time.

Since that time there have been no comptrollers; for the Earl of

---

prime gentlemen then about *London* being invited thither. Truly, he was a most compleat and well-accomplished gentleman, modest and court-like, and of so fair a demeanour, as made him be generally beloved; and for his wisdom, I shall give you but one character for all. He was ever great with all the favourites of his time, and although the king did often change, yet he was (*semper eidem*) with the king and favourites, and got by both; for although favourites had that exorbitant power over the king to make him grace and disgrace whom they pleased, he was out of that power, and the only exception to that general rule, and for his gettings, it was more than almost all the favourites of his time, which appeared in those vast expenses of all sorts, and had not the bounty of his mind exceeded his gettings, he might have left the greatest estate that ever our age or climate had heard of; he was indeed made for a courtier, who wholly studied his master, and understood him better than any other. He was employed in very many of the most weighty affairs, and sent with the most stately embassies of our times, which he performed with that wisdom and magnificency that he seemed an honour to his king and country for his carriage in State affairs." Through the influence of his royal master, Hay obtained in marriage Honora, only daughter and heiress of Edward, Lord Denny, and had a grant of the title of Lord Hay, with precedence next to the barons of England. On the 29th June, 1615, he was created a baron of the realm under the title of Lord Hay, of Sauley, Yorkshire. During the following year he was sent ambassador to the court of France. In March, 1617, he was sworn of the Privy Council, and on the 5th July, 1618, created Viscount Doncaster. In September, 1622, he was advanced to the earldom of Carlisle. He held various appointments at the court of James VI. He afterwards became first Gentleman of the Bedchamber to Charles I. He married, secondly, the Lady Lucy Percy, youngest daughter of Henry, Earl of Northumberland. He died 25th April, 1636, and was succeeded by James, his only surrviving son, who became second Earl of Carlisle. By his death in 1660, without issue, the earldom became extinct.— *Burke's Dormant and Extinct Peerage.*

Dunbar got comptrollery, collectory, and the treasury of the new augmentations, engrossed with the office of treasury in his gift, pretending it would be less charges to the king to pay one than four officers.

ADMIRALS.

1. James Hepburn, Earl of Bothwell,* great-grandson to Patrick, Lord Hales, who, in the parliament of King James IV., got for good service the lordship of Crichton, then being in his Majesty's hands by Lord Crichton's forfeiture, and the lordship of Bothwell, also being in his Majesty's hand by the forfeiture of John Ramsay, late Earl of Bothwell.

He it was, who after he had murdered Henry Stewart, father to King James VI., and had married Queen Mary, his mother, was declared by the estates a traitor, and pursued at their command by sea to Orkney, from whence he fled to Denmark, and there, being accused by the merchants, was imprisoned; and after ten years miserable captivity, died betwixt four walls, and by his death extinguished his posterity, and lost their honour for ever.

* James Hepburn, Earl of Bothwell, afterwards Duke of Orkney, was born about 1536, and succeeded his father in 1556. Though professedly a Protestant, he joined Mary of Guise against the Lords of Congregation, and proceeding to France recommended himself to Queen Mary. He was banished from Scotland in 1563 for conspiring against the Earl of Murray, but returned in 1565 when Murray was expatriated for opposing the queen's marriage with Darnley. After the murder of Rizzio he acquired the unbounded confidence of the queen, who appointed him Warden of the three Marches and Admiral of the kingdom. In the murder of Darnley, which took place on the 10th February, 1567, he was the principal agent. Being tried for the crime, he overawed his accusers by a powerful retinue, and was consequently acquitted. The queen now appointed him Governor of Edinburgh Castle, and captain of the Castle of Dunbar. By threats and promises he procured the consent of the leading nobility to his marriage with the queen, and having divorced his wife, Lady Jean Gordon, he was as Duke of Orkney married to Queen Mary on the 15th of May. On the 15th June the forces of the lords, confederated for the support of the young prince, met the followers of the queen and Bothwell at Carberry Hill. A conference took place between the queen and some of the confederated lords, when Bothwell rode off the field. He afterwards escaped to Orkney. For a time he subsisted by piracy, but pursued by a fleet, he fled to Norway. From thence he proceeded to Denmark, where being recognised, he was imprisoned in the castle of Draxholm. There he died on the 14th April, 1578.

2. Francis Stewart, Earl of Bothwell,* son to John Stewart, one of King James V.'s base sons, whom first he made Abbot of Kelso, by the counsel of Mr. John Mair, rector of the University of St. Andrews, whom that king met one day in the fields, and, not being known to be the king, was advised by him to make all his bastards priests, that they might not have children to trouble the state of the land. King James VI. bestowed on him the earldom of Bothwell, and made him admiral in Scotland.

He, in all his time grieving that he had not that power in court that he thought his birth and place deserved, leapt out, and made sundry out-reds against the king; one in Falkland, and another near Edinburgh; for which he was justly forfeited, and expelled the country.

His estate and place of admiralty was then given to the Duke of Lennox; the estate he resigned to the laird of Buccleuch, but kept still the admiralty to himself. And Bothwell fled to Italy, where he died in great misery; yet his son Francis, after he had spent the estate of a noble lady, the Countess of Perth, whom he married a widow, and daughter of the Earl of Winton, attended on King Charles I. at England, and procured, by his importunity, that Francis Earl of Buccleuch and his curators should submit anent these lands of the lordship of Bothwell, then possessed by him as heir to his father; and, by his Majesty's decreet-arbitral, he got them all restored; but *male parta pejus dilabuntur;* for he never brooked them, nor was anything the richer, since they accresced to his creditors, and now are in possession of one Dr. Seaton. His eldest son Francis became a trooper in the late war; as for the other brother, John, who was Abbot of Coldingham, he also disponed all that estate, and now has nothing, but lives on the charity of his friends.

3. Esme Stewart, Duke of Lennox,† was made admiral. He first married the widow of the sheriff of Ayr; but having small contentment in her, he quitted her at King James VI.'s going to England,

---

* John Stewart, Abbot of Kelso, was illegitimate son of James V. by Jane Hepburn, daughter of Patrick, Earl of Bothwell. His son, Francis Stewart, was created Earl of Bothwell 29th July, 1576, and appointed Lord High Admiral. The extraordinary career of this most turbulent and unprincipled individual forms a remarkable chapter in Scottish family history. He died at Naples in 1624. (See Anderson's "Scottish Nation," i., 357.)

† See *supra.*

and when, some few years thereafter, she followed him up to London, he sent her back again with small contentment. After that, she dying of displeasure, he married the Countess of Hereford, but had no children by her, and died suddenly in his bed, the first day of King James VI.'s last parliament, and was thought to have been poisoned.

4. Lewis,* son to Esme, Duke of Lennox, succeeded him in the honour and office of admiralty, and survived him scarce a year or two; but it was thought he was also poisoned, leaving his son James to be heir of the family. His relict, the Lord Clifford's daughter, being married to the Earl of Abercorn, came to Scotland, but that estate is now also totally disponed betwixt the Viscount of Kingston and the Lord Cochran.

5. John, Earl of Linlithgow,† having the full deputation of that place from both the brethren, and exercise of it many years, since that time has fallen from his own estate, and left nothing undisponed.

6. James, Duke of Lennox, son to Lewis,‡ albeit he had the title of admiral as successor to his progenitors, yet lost it by the English their incoming to Scotland, and their apprehending possession of the whole offices pertaining to the Crown, whereof that was one.

---

* Ludovick, second Duke of Lennox, was born 29th September, 1574. He was, though in his fifteenth year, appointed Governor of the east parts of Scotland during the absence of James VI. in Denmark in October, 1589. By marrying in 1591 Jane Ruthven, daughter of the Earl of Gowrie, he incurred the displeasure of the king, but was afterwards forgiven. He was appointed High Admiral in place of the Earl of Bothwell, and in 1598 was sworn of the Privy Council. He aided in rescuing the king from the Gowrie conspirators in 1600. After obtaining various offices and honours, he was in May, 1623, created Earl of Newcastle and Duke of Richmond in the peerage of England. He was found dead in his bed on the morning of the 16th February, 1624.

† Our author must mean either John, Master of Livingston, who died unmarried, or Alexander, second Earl of Linlithgow. The reference is obscure.

‡ James, fourth Duke of Lennox, was son of Esme, third duke, and not of the second duke as our author has stated. He was born 6th April, 1612, and succeeded his father at the age of twelve. In 1641 he was advanced to the Dukedom of Richmond. He was Lord Chamberlain and Admiral of Scotland, Lord Steward of the Household, Warden of the Cinque Ports, Gentleman of the Bedchamber, and a Knight of the Garter. During the Civil Wars he subscribed £40,000 in support of the royal cause. He died 30th March, 1655.

CHIEF JUSTICES.

1. William, Earl of Menteith,* was made chief-justice by King Charles I., after the said office had been demitted in his Majesty's hands by the Marquis of Argyle, who had the same heritably by patent from the king's predecessors. Menteith possessed the same till he was accused of misdemeanour to his Majesty, for his presumption to serve himself heir to the eldest son of Robert II., king of Scotland; and for making a renunciation of his title, with reservation of his blood, and saying he had the reddest blood of Scotland, he was dispossessed of all his places of council, session and exchequer, and chief justice, and sent home to be confined in his isle of Menteith, where he has still remained since.

His eldest son and apparent heir, the Lord Kilpunt,† being with James Graham in the time of the late troubles, was stabbed with a dirk by one Alexander Stewart; and his lady, daughter to the Earl Marischal, was distracted in her wits four years after, and his second son Sir James lies prisoner in England.

And albeit the said earl has got above £15,000 sterling from the king in the time of his flourishing, yet that is gone and exhausted,

* William Graham, sixth Earl of Menteith, by Mary, daughter of Sir Colin Campbell, of Glenurchy, succeeded his father in 1598. He was highly favoured by Charles I., who appointed him a Privy Councillor and Justice-General. He became President of the Privy Council, and in November, 1628, was nominated an Extraordinary Lord of Session. On the 25th August, 1630, he served himself heir to David, Earl of Strathern, and assumed the style of Earl of Strathern and Menteith. As David, Earl of Strathern, was eldest son of Robert II. by Euphemia Ross, and as at that period the priority of the king's marriage with Elizabeth More, mother of Robert III., was not established, the earl's procedure was unwise, and savoured of disloyalty. The king's attention being directed to the matter by Drummond, of Hawthornden, he caused the earl's retour and patent to be reduced, but soon afterwards bestowed on him the title of Earl of Airth and Menteith. In 1644 Lord Airth subscribed the Covenant, and was nominated on the Committee of War. His latter years were spent in retirement. (Brunton and Haig, Pinkerton's Scottish Gallery.)

† Lord Kilpont was an associate in arms of the Marquis of Montrose; he was stabbed to the heart in a sudden ebullition of passion by James Alexander (not Stewart), of Ardvoirlich, when Montrose with his army lay encamped at Collace after the battle of Tippermuir. The event has been embodied with fictitious colouring by Sir Walter Scott in the *Legend of Montrose*. In the introduction to that romance there is an interesting narrative respecting the unhappy author of the assassination and the circumstances connected with it. The estate of Kilpont, or Kilpunt, is situated near the river Almond, Linlithgowshire.

and still his estate is so much overcharged with debt, that it is feared his family shall end with him.

2. To him succeeded Sir William Elphinston,[*] brother to Sir George, who was justice-clerk; in his youth he had been a professor of philosophy in Nerac in France, and there studied the laws; then being in England, he was made secretary to Lady Elizabeth, when she was married to the Palatine; but within a few years he returned back to England, and got a place in the king's privy chamber; but, wearying of that employment, the king gave him a vacant place in the session, and made him lord chief justice, which place he enjoyed not above two or three years, and had neither lands nor personal estate in Scotland. When the troubles began, he went back to England, and there died in a hard condition, as may be supposed, the king being unable to help him.

III. After him † the Earl of Glencairn was made Chief Justice, and got a pension; but in few years he was displaced by authority of the Parliament, for being accessory to the engagement against England; and his estate by this means being much harmed, he was moved for eschewing of captions, to accept upon him the place of general of the forces that rose in the North against the English in 1653. What success he will have time will show.

The Office of Director of the Chancery.

Albeit in all times bypast it has been an office of state, and at his Majesty's disposal; yet partly by malice, but chiefly by ignorance, it

---

[*] Sir William Elphinstone was youngest son of George Elphinstone, of Blythswood. He was admitted an ordinary Lord of Session 1st March, 1637, and on the deprivation of the Earl of Menteith was appointed Justice-General. Of that office he was deprived in 1641, when the judges were chosen by the king with consent of the Estates. (Brunton and Haig.)

† After Sir William Elphinstone, Sir Thomas Hope, of Kerse, was Lord Justice-General; he died 23rd August, 1643. To him succeeded William, ninth Earl of Glencairn, whose appointment was ratified by the Estates 14th January, 1647. For supporting the "engagement" in 1648, he was in the following year deprived by Act of Classes. He raised the royal standard in the Highlands in 1653, but not long afterwards surrendered to Middleton. After the Restoration he waited on Charles II. at London, by whom he was nominated Lord High Chancellor. He advised the restoration of episcopacy, but was disgusted by the arrogant assumption of the primate, Archbishop Sharpe. He died 13th May, 1664, in his fifty-fourth year. (Brunton and Haig, 349.)

was, at the English coming to Scotland in the year 1650, holden and reputed an office subservient to the college of justice; and Sir John Scot, then director, displaced, and Alexander Jaffray, provost of Aberdeen, placed in his room, who then was an independent, and hereafter a quaker.

The Director, near these hundred years bygone, has been of the name of Scot, viz., since the year 1577. The first of that name was Robert Scot.* Mr. Robert, his son, got the place in 1582, but being hectic, resigned the place again to his father. Robert, then being old, resigned the place in 1592 in favour of the said Sir John, his grandchild, to his wife's son, Mr. William Scot (whose father was a maltman at the Westport; but his wife being left a rich widow, the said Robert married her, and only begot the said Sir John's father on her), and took a bond from the said Mr. William, to resign the place to the said Sir John when he was major, to which bond were witnesses inserted Adam Lawtie and Adam Cowpar, both writers to the signet. This bond at his death was consigned in the hands of Alexander Hay, Clerk Register, as the said Adam Cowpar, then clerk of the bills, informed Sir John, when he was major. Yet Mr. William, having got the bond from Alexander Hay, the said Alexander Hay's son, then a Clerk of the Session, caused his servant, Mr. Robert Williamson, put the same in the fire; who himself, in his sister's house in Conn's Close, burnt his own head of an apoplexy before any came near him.† And Mr. William, denying to the auditors of his and Sir John's accompts that ever there was such a bond, Sir John behoved to quit above 100,000 merks of his bygone rents, to get access to his grandfather's office, and he only to resign to Sir John his own place.

Sir James, Sir John's son, being joined in the place with his father by King Charles I., died in the year 1650.

Mr. William, at the time of his first marriage, having married the goodman of Priestfield's daughter, had not 500 merks to countervail his wife's tocher; yet thereafter Sir John, being curator *sine quo non* to his son of his last marriage, made him compt in presence of the Earl of Haddington, and Mr. William (*Hamilton*), his good-brother, for £1,000 *sterling* for a year's rent of his estate, by and attour five hundred bolls of bear that his mother had of conjunct-fee. The said

* *Vide* page 99. † *Vide* page 100.

Mr. William was thrice married, first to Elizabeth Hamilton, Priestfield's daughter, of whom was begotten Mr. John Scot, who being very learned, and author of a poesy to King James, printed in the Scots poets, was by his father sent to Rochelle to profess humanity, and there died of the plague. His second wife was Isobel Durie, daughter to the Laird of Durie, of whom he had a son, who, after he was married to Moncrieff's daughter, died childless; and his sister, who was crooked, was married to one Swinton, a sadler in Pittenweem. His last wife was Dame Jane Skene, whose posterity now succeeds. But if it be well conquest, posterity will be judge.

Sir John was a counsellor to King James and King Charles I., and Lord of Exchequer and a Lord of Session. Albeit he was possessor of the said place of chancery above forty years, and doer of great services to the king and country, yet, by the power and malice of his enemies, he has been at last thrust out of the said places in his old age, and likeways fined in £500 *sterling*, and one altogether unskilled placed to be director.* But as one of the ancients says well, *Ubi beneficia modum excesserunt, pro beneficio damnum rependitur;* "where benefits exceed measure, instead of benefits they get skaith." He had been a counsellor since the year of God 1620, and, for his Majesty's and predecessor's service, been twenty-four times at London, being 14,400 miles, and twice in the Low Countries, for printing the Scots poets, and the Atlas; and paid to John Bleau a hundred double pieces for printing the poets.

* Viz., Sir William Ker, who, as Sir John was pleased to say, danced him out of his office, being a dexterous dancer.—*Goodal.*

LIST OF THE GREAT OFFICERS OF STATE OF SCOTLAND, TO THE YEAR 1660.

CHANCELLORS.

EUAN, Chancellor to King Malcolm III., surnamed Kenmore, about the year	1057
Oswald, to King Donald VII.	1093
Earl Constantine, to Duncan II., the usurper	1094
Sphothad, Abbot of the religious Culdees, to Duncan	1094
Earl Rorey, to Donald VII. after the expulsion of Duncan	1097
Humphrey, Bishop of Dunkeld, to Edgar	1098
Constantine, Earl of Fife, to Alexander I.	1107
Herbert, Abbot and Bishop of Glasgow, to Alexander I.	1124
—— to David I.	1124
Walter, to David I.	1123
John, Bishop of Glasgow, *eod. reg.*	1129
Herbert, promoted from the office of Great Chamberlain to be Chancellor, *anno*	1129
Edward	1147
William Cumming, Bishop of Durham	
Henry, Earl of Northumberland	
Engelramus, Bishop of Glasgow, *eod. reg.*	1151
—— to Malcolm IV., 1154.	
Walterus Senescallus, to David I.	1153
—— to Malcolm IV.	1155
Christopher, Bishop of Dunkeld, *eod. reg.*	1157
Nicolaus, Chamberlain and Chancellor, *eod. reg.*	1161
—— to King William, 1179.	
Willielmus de Ripariis, Prior of St. Andrews	1163
Hugo de Morville, Lord Lauderdale, to King William, *anno* 1mo regni.	1165

Walter Bidun, Bishop elect of Dunkeld, to King William	1171
Roger, son to the Earl of Leicester, Bishop of St. Andrews, *cod. reg.*	1178
Walterus de Beide, a Frenchman, *cod. reg.*	1183
Walterus de Vidone, *cod. reg.*	1187
Hugo, Bishop of Glasgow, *cod. reg.*	1189
Willielmus de Lundyne	1192
William Malvicine, Bishop of St. Andrews, *cod. reg.*	1199
Florence, Bishop elect of Glasgow, *cod. reg.*	1202
Richardus, thereafter Bishop of Dunkeld, *cod. reg.*	
Willielmus de Bosco, or Wood, Bishop of Dumblane, *cod. reg.*	1211
—— to Alexander II., 1226.	
Florentine, Bishop elect of Glasgow	1213
Willielmus de Riddel	1214
Robert Kildelicht, Abbot of Dunfermline, to Alexander II.	1214
—— to Alexander III., *anno* 1249.	
Walterus de Olifard, to Alexander II.	1216
Thomas de Strivelyn, Archdeacon of Glasgow, to Alexander II.	1226
Matthew Scot, Bishop of Aberdeen	1227
William de Lindesay	1230
William Babington, or Bondington, Bishop of Glasgow	1231
Bernard of Innerkeithing, Bishop of Dumblane	
William de Huntingdon	1231
William de Bond, *cod. reg.*	1247
Gameline, Bishop of St. Andrews, *cod. reg.*	
—— to Alexander III.	1251
Richard of Innerkeithing, Bishop of Dunkeld, to Alexander III.	1253
William Vitchard, or Wishart, Bishop of Glasgow, thereafter of St. Andrews, *cod. reg.*	1256
William Fraser, Dean of Glasgow, thereafter Bishop of St. Andrews, *cod. reg.*	1273
—— to John Baliol	1295
Alexander de Baliol, *cod. reg.*	1295
Allan, Bishop of Caithness, *cod. reg.*, and confirmed in the office by Edward I. of England, as Superior.	
Maurice, Bishop of the Isles, *cod. reg.*	1298
Adam, Bishop of Brechin, *cod. reg.*, and afterwards in the reign of David II.	

LIST OF THE GREAT OFFICERS OF STATE: 125

Bernard, Abbot of Arbroath, to Robert Bruce, from 1301 to his death in 1327
Dr. Walter Twynham, Canon of Glagsow, *cod. reg.* . . 1327
Patrick Leuchars, Bishop of Brechin, to David II. . . 1345
—— a second time, 1367.
Thomas de Carnotto, or Charters, de Kinfawns, *cod. reg.* 1347
Mr. William Caldwell, Prebend of Glasgow 1349
Sir John Carrick, Canon of Glasgow, to David II., and thereafter to Robert II., after Lord Glammis.
John Peebles, Bishop elect of Dunkeld, *cod. reg.* . . . 1377
John Lyon, Lord Glammis, *cod. reg.* 1380
Sir Alexander Cockburn, of Langton, to Robert III. . . 1395
Robert Lord Boyd, *cod. reg.*
Mr. Duncan Petit, Archbishop of Glasgow.
Gilbert Greenlaw, Bishop of Aberdeen, to Robert III., and during the government of Robert and Murdo, Dukes of Albany, regents.
Sir John Forrester, of Costerphin, to James I. . . . 1425
William Lauder, Bishop of Glasgow, *cod. reg.* . . . 1424
John Cameron, Bishop of Glasgow, *cod. reg.* . . . 1427
Sir William Crichton, knight, afterwards Lord Crichton, *cod. reg.*, and in the reign of James II. He was turned out in 1444, but got the office again after the death of Bishop Bruce in 1447, and kept it till his death in 1455.
James Kennedy, Bishop of St. Andrews, succeeded Crichton in 1444, but held the place only a few weeks.
James Bruce, Bishop of Dunkeld, and afterwards of Glasgow, to James II., *anno* 1444
William Sinclair, Earl of Orkney and Caithness, *cod. reg.* . 1455
—— to James III.
George Shoriswood, Bishop of Brechin, *cod. reg.* . . . 1458
Robert, Lord Boyd, to James III., according to Buchanan 1460
Andrew Stewart, Lord Evandale, *cod. reg.* 1460
John Lang, Bishop of Glasgow, *cod. reg.* 1482
James Livington, Bishop of Dunkeld, *cod. reg.* . . . 1483
Colin, Earl of Argyle, *cod. reg.* 1484
Colin, Earl of Argyle, to James IV., 1490.
William Elphinston, Bishop of Aberdeen, at the death of James III. 1485

Archibald, Earl of Angus, to James IV.   .   .   1493
George Gordon, Earl of Huntly, *cod. reg.*   .   .   .   1498
James Stuart, Duke of Ross, Archbishop of St. Andrews,
    second son to James III., *cod. reg.*   1500
Andrew Foreman, Archbishop of St. Andrews, *eod. reg.*
Alexander Stewart, Archbishop of St. Andrews, natural son
    to James IV., *eod. reg.*   1510
James Beaton, Archbishop of St. Andrews, *cod. reg.*   .   .   1512
—— to James V.   1515
Archibald Douglas, Earl of Angus, husband to the Queen
    Dowager, *cod. reg.*   1525
Gavin Dunbar, Archbishop of Glasgow, and afterwards of
    St. Andrews, tutor to James V.   1528
William Stuart, Bishop of Aberdeen   1546
David Beaton, Cardinal and Archbishop of St. Andrews, in
    the reign of Q. Mary.
John Hamilton, Archbishop of St. Andrews, *cod. reg.*
George Gordon, second Earl of Huntly   1561
Monsieur Ruby, a French lawyer, put in for a little time by
    the Queen Regent.
James Douglas, Earl of Morton   1562
George, third Earl of Huntly   1567
James, Earl of Morton, made Chancellor a second time   .   1567
Archibald, Earl of Argyle   1572
John, Lord Glammis   1573
John Stuart, Earl of Athole   1578
Colin, Earl of Argyle   1579
James Stuart, Earl of Arran   1584
Sir John Maitland, of Lethington, Lord Thirlestaine   .   .   1585
John Graham, Earl of Montrose   1597
Alexander Seton, Earl of Dunfermline   1605
Sir George Hay, of Nertherlieffe, Earl of Kinnoul   .   .   1622
John Spottiswood, Archbishop of St. Andrews   .   .   1634
John Campbell, of Lauers, Earl of Loudoun .   .   .   1641
William Cunningham, Earl of Glencairn   .   .   .   1660

TREASURERS.

Sir Walter Ogilby, of Lintrethan, to K. James I.   .   .   1420
Patrick de Ogilby   1430

Thomas de Mirton, Deacon of Glasgow.
Walter de Haliburton 1439
Robert Livingston, son to the governor.
Wal. Halyburton, to James II. 1440
Andrew, Abbot of Melross, *cod. reg.* 1449
Mr. James Stewart, Dean of Moray, *cod. reg.* . . . 1455
Mr. David Guthrie, to James III. 1466
William Knowlis, Preceptor of Torpichen . . . 1470
John Laing, Parson of Kenland 1473
Archibald Crawfurd, Abbot of Holyrood House . . 1480
Sir John Ramsay, of Balmaine.
Henry, Abbot of Cambuskenneth, to James IV. . . 1490
George, Abbot of Dunfermline 1493
George, Abbot of Paisley 1495
Robert Lundy, of Balgony 1499
James Beaton, then Abbot of Dunfermline, thereafter Archbishop of St. Andrews 1507
George, Abbot of Arbroath 1509
Andrew, Bishop of Caithness 1509
James, Archbishop of Glasgow 1510
William, Lord St. John, of Torpichen 1512
Mr. John Campbell, of Lundie 1517
Archibald Douglas, of Kilspindie 1520
Archibald Douglas, Provost of Edinburgh . . . 1527
Robert Barton, of Over-barnton 1528
William Elphingston, Bishop of Aberdeen . . . 1533
Robert, Abbot of Holyrood House 1537
James, Abbot of Paisley, when James V. died . . 1543
John Hamilton, brother to the regent, Abbot of Paisley, and afterwards Archbishop of St. Andrews, Treasurer in Q. Mary's minority 1546
James Kirkaldy, of Grange 1548
Gilbert Kennedy, Earl of Cassilis 1555
Mr. Robert Richardson, Commendat. of St. Mary's Isle . 1561
Mr. William Stewart, Provost of Lincluden . . . 1564
William, Earl of Gowry 1572
John, Earl of Montrose 1584
Sir Thomas Lyon, of Auld-bar, Master of Glammis . 1585
Walter Stewart, Lord Blantyre 1595

128   LIST OF THE GREAT OFFICERS OF STATE.

Alexander, Lord Elphingston 1599
Sir George Hume, Earl of Dunbar 1601
Robert Ker, Earl of Somerset 1611
John Erskine, Earl of Mar 1616
William Douglas, Earl of Morton 1630
John Stewart, Earl of Traquair, in 1636, promoted from Depute Treasurer to be Principal Treasurer, which he kept till 1641

John, Earl of Loudoun, then Chancellor.
Archibald, Marquis of Argyle.
William, Earl of Glencairn.
John, Earl of Lindsay.
Sir James Carmichael, Treasurer Depute.
These five were, by the Parliament 1641, appointed Commissioners for managing the Treasury, after Traquair was cashiered and indicted for high treason, and to endure till the next Parliament.

John, Earl of Crawfurd and Lindsay, made Treasurer by the States in 1641, but turned out for his adhering to the engagement in 1649, and reponed by K. Charles in   1660
And the office was again, in 1649, put in the hands of Commissioners, who were,
John, Earl of Loudoun, Chancellor.
Archibald, Marquis of Argyle.
Alexander, Earl of Eglinton.
John, Earl of Cassilis.
Robert, Lord Burleigh.
Sir Daniel Carmichael, Treasurer Depute.

TREASURER DEPUTES.

Sir Robert Melvil, of Mordecairny, afterwards Lord Melvil, first Treasurer Depute 1582
Sir John Arnot, of Bersick 1604
Sir Gideon Murray, of Elibank 1613
Sir Archibald Napier, of Merchiston, afterwards Lord Napier 1623
John Stuart, Lord Traquair 1630
Sir James Carmichael, of that ilk   1637

LIST OF THE GREAT OFFICERS OF STATE.

Sir Daniel Carmichael, third son to Sir James, put in by the
Parliament in 1649
William, Lord Ballenden, of Bruchton 1661

COMPTROLLERS.

David Brune, Comptroller of the House 1426
John Spence 1429
Alexander de Nairne, of Sanford 1446
Robert de Livingston 1448
Ninian Spot, Canon of Dunkeld and Moray . . . 1458
John Colquhoun, of that ilk 1464
David Guthrie, of that ilk 1467
Adam Wallace, of Craigie 1468
James Schaw de Salquhy 1471
Thomas Simson 1472
Alexander Lesly de Warderis.
Alexander Inglis, Archdeacon of St. Andrews . . . 1488
Patrick Hume de Polwart 1499
James Abbot, of Dunfermline 1506
James Riddoch, of Aberladenoche 1507
Robert Arnot, of Woodmill, killed at Flowden . . . 1513
Duncan Forrester de Carden 1514
Patrick Hamilton 1515
Alexander Garden 1516
Robert Burton, of Overbarton 1520
Sir James Colvil, of Ochiltree 1525
David Wood, of Craig 1538
Thomas Menzies 1543
William Commendator de Culross 1546
William, Abbot of Ross 1548
Monsieur de Ruby, to Q. Mary the Regent . . . 1557
Bartholomew Villemore, to the household, named, but never
exercised 1560
Sir John Wishart, of Pittarrow 1561
Sir William Murray, of Tullibarden 1563
James Cockburn, of Skirling 1567
Sir James Campbell, of Ardkinglass 1584
Andrew Wood, of Largo 1585
David Seton, of Parbroath 1589

Walter, Prior of Blantyre 1597
Sir George Hume, of Wedderburn 1599
Sir David Murray, of Gospetrie, afterwards Lord Scone. . 1600
Peter, Bishop of Dunkeld 1603
Sir James Hay, of Fingask 1610
Sir Gideon Murray, of Elibank, was the last Comptroller to James VI., in whose time the office was suppressed, and incorporated with that of the great Treasurer . . 1615

The Lords of Privy Seal.

Walter Foote, Provost of Bothwell, *Secreti Sigilli Custos* to K. James I. 1424
Mr. John Cameron, Provost of Lincluden, and Bishop of Glasgow 1426
Mr. William Foulis, Provost of Bothwell 1432
Mr. William Turnbull, Canon of Glasgow, to James II. . 1442
Thomas, Bishop of Galloway 1458
Mr. John Arouse 1459
Mr. James Lindsay, Provost of Lincluden . . . 1463
Thomas Spence, Bishop of Aberdeen, to James III. . . 1467
William Tulloch, Bishop of Orkney 1470
William Tulloch, Bishop of Moray 1477
Andrew Stewart, Bishop Elect of Moray, brother uterine to James III. 1482
Mr. David Livingston, Rector de Air, and Provost of Lincluden 1482
John, Prior of St. Andrews, to James IV. . . . 1489
William Elphinston, Bishop of Aberdeen 1500
Alexander Gordon, Bishop of Aberdeen 1507
David, Abbot of Arbroath, to James V. 1514
George, Abbot of Holyrood House 1519
George, Bishop of Dunkeld 1526
Archbishop Douglas, of Kilspindie 1527
Robert Colvil, of Crawford, one of the Senators of the College of Justice.
David Beaton, Abbot of Arbroath, Cardinal and Archbishop of St. Andrews 1542
John Hamilton, Abbot of Paisley, and Archbishop of St. Andrews 1542

LIST OF THE GREAT OFFICERS OF STATE.

George, Earl of Dunfermline 1553
Sir Richard Maitland, of Lethington 1563
John Maitland, Prior of Coldingham 1567
Mr. George Buchanan, a Lord of the Session, and Privy Councillor, Commendator of Crossraguel, and Preceptor to the King 1571
Walter Stuart, Commendator and Prior of Blantyre . . 1583
Sir Richard Cockburn, of Clerkington 1595
Thomas, Earl of Haddington 1626
Robert, Earl of Roxburgh 1641
Jo. Gordon, Earl of Sutherland, had the office conferred on him by the Parliament 1649
Charles, Earl of Dunfermline 1661

SECRETARIES.

Nicolaus, in the reign of Malcolm IV., Duncan Pecoce, to Robert II. 1380
Andrew de Hawick, Rector de Liston 1410
John, Earl of Buchan 1418
Mr. John Cameron, afterwards Bishop of Glasgow, Secretary to James I. 1424
Mr. William Foulis 1429
Mr. John Methven 1432
John, Bishop of Dunkeld, to James II. 1448
William Otterburne 1452
George de Shoriswood 1453
John Arouse, Archdeacon of Glasgow 1454
Thomas de Vans, Deacon of Glasgow.
Mr. James Law, Archdeacon of Glasgow 1463
Mr. Archibald Whitlaw, Archdeacon of Glasgow, and then Archdeacon of Lothian 1463
Mr. Alexander Inglis, thereafter Bishop of Dunkeld . . 1488
Mr. Patrick Panter, Rector of Tarmadies, then Archdeacon of Murray, afterwards Abbot of Cambuskenneth, to King James IV. 1490
Mr. Richard Murehead, Dean of Glasgow, and also to K. James V., 1535 1495
Michael Balfour, Abbot of Melross 1496
Mr. Thomas Hay, to James V. 1516

Mr. Patrick Hepburn, Rector de Whiteston 1524
Mr. Thomas Erskin, of Halton, afterwards Sir Thomas
    Erskin, of Brechin 1524
Patrick, Abbot of Cambuskenneth 1528
Mr. David Panter, Bishop of Ross 1543
Mr. James Strachan, a Canon of Aberdeen.
David Rizzio, to Q. Mary 1559
Sir William Maitland, of Lethington, younger . . . 1561
Sir James Balfour, of Pittendreich, to Q. Mary . . . 1564
James Maxwell, of Cramond, son to Sir William Maxwell,
    to Q. Mary.
Mr. Robert Pitcairn, Advocate, Commendator of Dunfermline, and Archdeacon of St. Andrews 1572
Sir John Maitland, of Thirlestane 1584
Sir Richard Cockburn, of Clerkingtoun 1591
Sir John Lindsay, of Balcarras 1596
Mr. James Elphinstoun, of Innerneitie, Parson of Eglesham,
    and afterwards Lord Balmerino 1597
Sir Alexander Hay, of Newton, second son to Sir Alexander
    Hay, of Easter-Kennet 1608
Sir John Preston, President of the Session.
Sir Thomas Hamilton, Earl of Haddington 1612
    From him Charles I. took the Seals, and divided them,
      giving the one to—
Sir William Alexander, Earl of Stirling, and the other to } 1626
Sir Archibald Acheson, of Glencairn . . . . . }
William, Earl of Lanark, afterwards Duke of Hamilton. . 1641
Sir Robert Spottiswood, Lord New-Abbay, and President of
    the Session 1644
Sir William Ker, Earl of Lothian, made Secretary by the
    Parliament, when the Earl of Lanark fled for malignancy.
George, Earl of Seaforth, by Charles II. in Holland.

Clerks of Register.

William, Bishop of St. Andrews.
Simon de Quincy.
Nicolaus, *Clericus* to Malcolm IV.
William de Bosch, and one Hugo.
Galfrid and Gregory, to Alexander II.

LIST OF THE GREAT OFFICERS OF STATE.

Willielmus Capellanus, and Alexander de Carrerg . 1253
All these were called *cler. dom. regis.*
Robert de Dunbar, *cler. rotul.* 1323
John Gray to Robert II.
John Schives, *Decretorum Director* 1426
Richard Craig, Vic. de Dundee 1440
George Shoriswood, Rector de Cutler 1442
Sir John Methven 1449
Mr. John Arouse, Archdeacon of Glasgow . . . 1450
Mr. Nicol Otterburn 1455
Fergus M'Dowall 1466
Mr. David Guthrie, of that ilk 1471
John Layng, Rector de Newlands 1473
Alexander Inglis, *Cancel. Aberdon.*, afterwards Deacon of
    Dunkeld 1477
Patrick Leith, Canon of Glasgow 1482
Alexander Scot, Rector de Wigton 1482
William Hepburn, Vic. de Linlithgow 1488
Richard Murehead, Deacon of Glasgow . . . 1489
John Fraser, Rector de Restalrig 1492
Walter Drummond, Deacon of Dumblane . . . 1497
Mr. Gavin Dumbar, Archdeacon of St. Andrews, afterwards
    Bishop of Aberdeen 1500
Sir Stephen Lockhart, to James IV.
Sir James Foulis, of Colington 1531
Sir Thomas Marjoribanks, of Ratho 1548
Mr. James M'Gill, of Rankeilor, Parson of Flisk . . 1554
    Turned out for D. Rizzio's murder in 1565, restored 1567,
    and continued to 1677.
Sir James Balfour, of Pittendreich, Rector of Flisk . . 1565
Sir Alexander Hay, of Easter-Kennet 1577
Sir John Skeen, of Currie Hill 1594
Mr. James Skeen, conjunct with his father . . . 1598
Sir Thomas Hamilton, afterwards Earl of Haddington . 1612
Sir Alexander Hay, of Whitburgh 1612
Sir George Hay, of Netherleiffe 1616
Sir John Hamilton of Magdalens, brother to the Earl of
    Haddington 1622
Sir John Hay, of Lands 1632

134   LIST OF THE GREAT OFFICERS OF STATE.

Sir Alexander Gibson, younger of Durie . . . 1641
Sir Archibald Johnstoun, of Warriston 1649
Sir Archibald Primrose, of Chester 1660

Lord Chief Justices.

Argadus, Captain of Argyle, in the reign of Ethodius.
Comes Dunetus, in the reign of K. William.
The Earl of Fife, *eod. reg.*
William Cummin, *eod. reg.*
David, Earl of Huntingdon, *eod. reg.*
Walter Cliffer, *eod. reg. justit. Laudoniæ.*
Allan, to Alexander II. 1216
William Cummin, Earl of Buchan, *eod. reg.* . . . 1224
Walter Oliphant, of Olifard, *eod. reg.* 1227
Walter, son to Allan, Seneschal or Stewart of Scotland, *eod. reg.*
William, Earl of Ross, Lord Chief Justice, *ex parte boreali maris Scoticani* 1239
David de Lindsay, *justit. Laudoniæ* 1243
Alexander Seneschal, to Alexander II.
Hugo de Berclay, *justit. Laudoniæ, eod. reg.*
Alexander Cummin, Earl of Buchan, to Alexander III. . 1253
Robert de Erskin, *ex parte boreali de Forth*, to David II. . 1366
Robert de Lauder, *justit. ex parte boreali aquæ de Forth, de Edrington & Bass* 1426
Patrick de Ogilvy, *justit. ex parte boreali aquæ de Forth*, to James I. 1446
John, Lord Lindsay de Bayrs, *ex parte boreali aquæ de Forth* . 1475
William, Earl of Orkney, *ex parte Australi aquæ de Forth*, to James II.
John Haddin, of Glenegys, *justit. gen.* benorth Forth, to James III. 1477
Patrick Hepburn, Lord Hales, and Robert Lord Leyl, besouth Forth, *eod. reg.*
Andrew, Earl of Crawfurd, and the Earl of Huntly, benorth Forth, *eod. reg.*
Robert, Lord Leyl, Lord Chief Justice 1488
John, Lord Glammis, and John, Lord Drummond . . 1489
Robert, Lord Leyl, and John, Lord Glammis . 1492
John, Lord Drummond 1494

LIST OF THE GREAT OFFICERS OF STATE. 135

Andrew, Lord Gray, and John, Lord Kennedy . . . 1504
Colin, Earl of Argyle 1514
Archibald Douglas, of Kilspindie 1526
Archibald, Earl of Argyle 1537
Gilespick, Earl of Argyle, heritably 1567
Colin, Earl of Argyle 1578
Archibald, Earl of Argyle 1589
    He exchanged the office of Lord Chief Justice in 1607, for the heritable Lieutenancy of Argyle and Lorn, and most of the isles.
William, Earl of Menteith 1628
Sir William Elphinston.
Sir Thomas Hope, younger of Kerse 1642
William, Earl of Glencairn.
The Earl of Cassilis 1649

JUSTICE CLERKS.

William de Cameron, Justice Clerk to David II.
Adam Forrester, *eod. reg.*
William Halket, of Belfico 1478
Mr. Richard Lawson, of Heirigs 1491
Mr. James Henderson, of Fordel 1507
Mr. James Wishart, of Pitarrow 1513
Nicholas Crawfurd, of Oxengangs 1524
Mr. Adam Otterburn, of Redhall 1537
Thomas Scot, of Pitgorn 1537
Mr. Thomas Bellenden, of Achnoul 1539
Mr. Henry Balneaves 1540
Sir John Ballenden, of Achnoul 1547
Sir Lewis Ballenden, of Achnoul 1578
Sir John Cockburn, of Ormiston 1591
Sir George Elphinston, of Blythswood 1625
Sir James Carmichael, of that ilk 1634
Sir John Hamilton, of Orbiston 1637

KING'S ADVOCATES.

John Ross, of Mongrennan 1483
Mr. James Henderson, of Fordel 1494
Mr. Richard Lawson de Heirigs 1503

Mr. James Wishart, of Pitarrow 1513
Mr. Adam Otterburn, of Redhall 1525
Mr. John Fowler, or Fowlis, conjunct with Otterburn . . 1527
Mr. Henry Lauder, of St. Germains, conjunct with Otterburn
  after Fowlis 1533
Mr. Henry Balneaves, to Q. Mary.
Mr. Thos. Cummin, a Lord of Session, *eod. reg.*
Mr. John Spence, of Condie 1561
Mr. Robert Crichton, of Eliok 1561
Mr. David Borthwick, of Loch-hill 1573
Mr. David Macgill, of Cranston-riddel and Nisbet, son to Sir
  James, Clerk-Reg. 1582
Mr. John Skene 1589
Mr. William Hart, of Livelands 1594
Mr. Andrew Logie.
Mr. Thomas Hamilton, of Drumcarny, Monkland, and Binning,
  afterwards Earl of Haddington, conjoined with Mr. David
  Macgill, 1595, and afterwards sole Advocate.
Sir William Oliphant, of Newton 1612
Mr. Thomas Hope, of Craighall, afterwards Sir Thomas . 1626
Sir Archibald Johnston, of Warriston 1641
Sir Thomas Nicholson.

ADMIRALS.

Henry, Earl of Orkney, to Robert III.
George de Crichton de Carnes, who was Earl of Caithness, to
  James II., 1449 and 1452.
William, Earl of Caithness and Orkney, *cod. reg.*
David, Earl of Crawfurd, to James III. 1474
Alexander, Duke of Albany 1482
Andrew Wood, of Largo, was never admiral; but in 1477 was
  master of the *Yellow Carval;* and in James IV.'s time
  his son defended the castle of Dumbarton against the
  English before 1503; got Largo in 1477 to uphold his
  ship, and in 1482 got it in heritage *ex autographis.*
Patrick, Lord Bothwell 1501
James, Earl of Arran, *cod. reg.*
Archibald, Earl of Angus, *cod. reg.*
Robert, Lord Maxwell, to James V.

LIST OF THE GREAT OFFICERS OF STATE.

Adam, Earl of Bothwell, heritably 1511
Patrick, Earl of Bothwell 1544
James, Earl of Bothwell 1567
James, Earl of Morton 1578
Francis, Earl of Bothwell 1583
James, Duke of Lennox, heritably 1626
John, Earl of Linlithgow, made admiral during the Duke of Lennox's minority.
James, Duke of Lennox 1633
James, Duke of York, afterwards K. James VII.

DIRECTORS OF THE CHANCERY.

Walter, *Cler. cancellarii* 1159
Andrew Tailifer and William Cadyow, *cler. cancel.*. . . 1425
Mr. Richard Gray, *licen. in decret. cler. cancel.* . . . 1440
Mr. George Shorswood, of Cultrie 1451
Robert Colvil, of Ochiltree, Director of the Chancery . . 1508
Henry Stewart, afterwards Lord Methven 1523
Patrick Houston, of that ilk 1526
Sir James Colvil, of Ochiltree, afterwards of Easter-wemyss . 1529
Mr. James Ballenden, of Achnoul 1538
Mr. Thomas Ballenden, of Achnoul 1540
John Ballenden 1544
James Hamilton, of Stenhouse, and William Ogyl . . 1546
Alexander Livingston, of Dunipace . . 1548 & 1553
Mr. George Buchanan 1570
Alexander Hay 1574
Mr. Robert Scot 1577
Mr. William Scott, of Grangemuir, afterwards of Ardross . 1594
Mr. John Scot, of Caiplie, afterwards Sir John of Scotstarvet 1608

LORD CHAMBERLAINS.

Herbert, to David I. and to Malcolm IV. 1159
Nicolaus, *eod. reg.* 1179
Philip de Valenois, to K. William 1205
Walter de Barclay, *eod. reg.*
Hugo de Giffer, *eod. reg.*
John de Melvil, to Alexander II.
Henricus de Baliol, *eod. reg.* 1216

David de Benham, afterwards Bishop of St. Andrews, *eod. reg.* 1228
William, Earl of Mar, to Alexander III. 1253
Henry de Baliol, *eod. reg.* 1261
Joannes de Lindsay, *eod. reg.* 1278
William de Lindsay, to Robert I. 1319
Alexander Frazer, who married Mary Bruce, the king's sister,
   eod. reg. 1325
John Baptista, to David II. 1329
Robert de Peebles, *eod. reg.*
Thomas, Earl of Mar, *eod. reg.* 1349
Walter Fleming, of Biggar, *eod. reg.* 1350
Robert de Erskine, *eod. reg.* 1354
William de Biggar, Rector of the Church of Errol, to
   Robert II. 1371
Michael, Bishop of Dunkeld, *eod. reg.* 1376
John Lyon, *eod. reg.* 1378
John, Earl of Buchan, *eod. reg.*
John Forrester de Corstorphin, to James I. . . . 1426
George, Bishop of Brechin, *eod. reg.* 1431
James, Lord Livingstone, to James II. 1438
Lord Boyd, to James III.
James, Earl of Buchan, *eod. reg.* 1477
David, Earl of Crawfurd, *eod. reg.* 1483
Alexander, Lord Hume, to James IV. 1489
Malcolm, Lord Fleming, to James V. 1516
John Lord Fleming, to Q. Mary 1565
   He was also usher of the King's chamber.
Esme, Duke of Lennox, to James VI. 1581
Ludovick, Duke of Lennox, *eod. reg.* 1594
   He and his successors were made heritable chamberlains.

MASTERS OF THE KING'S HOUSEHOLD.

Walter de Ogilby de Lintrethan, to James I. . . . 1432
John, Lord Seton, *eod. reg.*
Patrick, Lord Glammis, to James II. 1450
Andrew, Lord Gray, *eod. reg.* 1452
Colin, Earl of Argyle, to James III. 1465
David, Earl of Crawford, *eod. reg.* 1482
William, Lord Borthwick, *eod. reg.* 1484

LIST OF THE GREAT OFFICERS OF STATE.

John Ramsay, *eod. reg.*
David, Earl of Crawfurd, *eod. reg.* 1488
Patrick, Lord Hales 1488
William Knolls, Lord St. John 1491
Andrew, Lord Gray 1492
Archibald, Earl of Argyle 1495
Lord Maxwell.
Colin, Earl of Argyle 1529
    This office continued afterwards heritably in that family.
The Earl of Mar was appointed Master of the Household
    for Prince Henry's christening 1594

KEEPERS OF THE GREAT SEAL.

Alexander Cockburn de Lantoun, to Robert III.
John Forrester de Corstorphin 1420
John Cameron, Bishop of Glasgow 1426
Monsieur Ruby 1560
David Rizzio 1564

MASTERS OF REQUESTS.

Mr. James Ogilby, Commendator of Dryburgh . . . 1515
Sir John Hay, Abbot of Dalmerino, Parson of Monimusk . 1554
Mr. Thomas Hepburn, Parson of Aulderstocks . . . 1567
Mr. James Colvil 1579
Mr. Mark Ker, son to the Abbot of Newbottle . . . 1592
William Ballenden, *Magis. Supplic. Libellar.* . . . 1608
Sir James Galloway, afterward Lord Dunkeld . . . 1624
Sir William Alexander, Earl of Stirling 1626
Sir John Chiesly 1648

CONSTABLES.

Hugo de Morville, to David I., Edward, *eod. reg.*
Richard de Morville, to Malcolm IV. 1163
William de Morville, his son.
Allan de Galloway, son to Rowland de Galloway and Helene
    Morville (sister to the last constable), to Alexander II.

Sir Leonard Leslie, to Alexander III.
Roger de Quincey, Earl of Winton, Constable by marrying the daughter of the Lord Galloway.
Scierus de Quincey, Earl of Winton, son to Roger, forfeited by Robert I.
Gilbert Hay, made heritable Constable and Earl of Errol . 1321
And that family has kept the office ever since.

INDEX.

Abercorn, Lord, 86.
Aboyne, Lord, 39.
Acheson, Sir Archibald, 77.
Admiral, Office of, 32.
Aikenhead, James, 50.
Aitchison, Alexander, of Gosford, 2.
Alexander, Sir William, 75—77.
Ancrum, Earl of, 90.
Angus, Earl of, 81.
Argyle, Colin, Earl of, 40.
Argyle, Marquis of, 6, 38, 41, 49.
Arnot, Sir John, 65.
Arran, Earl of, 37, 41, 42, 81, 85, 86.
Athole, John, Earl of, 39, 40, 42.

Baillie, Sir James, 57.
Balcarras, Lord, 70.
Balfour, David, 96.
Balfour, Sir James, 3, 13, 37, 96—98.
Balfour, Sir Michael, 96.
Balfour, Sir William, 51.
Ballantyne, Sir John, 104.
Ballantyne, Sir Lewis, 104.
Ballantyne, Thomas, 104.
Balmerino, Lords, 58, 71, 72.
Barlæus, Caspar, 3.
Barlæus, William, 3.
Beaton, Cardinal, 82, 93.
Bedford, Earls of, 58, 73.
Belhaven, Lord, 87.
Belshes, Advocate, 37.
Blantyre, William, Lord, 56.
Bleau, John, 4, 11—17, 122.
Bleau's Atlas, 11—17.
Borthwick, David, 70, 108.
Bothwell, Earls of, 84, 116, 117.
Boyd, The Lords, 80.
Buccleuch, Laird of, 117.
Buchanan, George, 93.
Burleigh, Laird of, 97.

Canning, Earl, 23.
Carlisle, Earls of, 48, 114, 115.
Carmichael, John, 50.
Carstairs, John, 105.
Cassilis, Earls of, 39, 81.
Cecil, Secretary, 57, 71.
Chamberlain, Office of Great, 29.

Chancellor, Office of the, 26.
Chancery, Directors of the, 3, 27.
Charles I., 5, 12.
Chatelherault, Duke of, 85.
Clemens, Antony, 3.
Cockburn, Sir John, 105.
Cockburn, Sir Richard, 94.
Constable, Office of, 30.
Crawford, Earls of, 39, 55, 63.
Crichton, Robert, 106.
Crichton, Sir Robert, 106.
Crichton, the Admirable, 106.

Dalziel, Sir Robert, 59.
Darnley, Lord, 85.
Dennie, Lord, 115.
Derby, Earl of, 90.
Dick, Sir William, Bart., 21.
Douglas, Sir Robert, 37.
Drummond, Lady Jean, 95.
Drummond, Sir John, 21.
Drummond, William, of Hawthornden, 18, 44.
Dunbar, Earl of, 57.
Duncan, Andrew, 50.
Dundas, Robert, of Arniston, 23.
Dunfermline, Earls of, 46, 47.
Durie, Robert, 50.

Elphinstone, Lords, 56, 70.
Elphinstone, Sir George, 105.
Elphinstone, Sir William, 120.

Forbes, John, 50.
Frendraught, Viscount, 107.

Gibson, Sir Alexander, 5, 101.
Gladstanes, Archbishop, 49.
Glammis, John, Lord, 39.
Glammis, Lord Chancellor, 55.
Glasgow, Sir John Scot's endowments at, 17, 18.
Glencairn, Earl of, 120.
Goldman, Peter, 3.
Gordon, Lord, 39.
Gordon, Lord George, 39.
Gordon, Rev. James, 12, 15.
Gordon, Robert, of Straloch, 11, 17.

Gordon, Sir Robert, Bart., 22.
Gowrie, Earl of, 53.
Graham, Richard, 104.
Grierson, Sir John, of Lag, 21.
Gruter, Isaac, 3, 4.

Haddington, Earls of, 58, 73, 75, 94, 100, 121.
Hamilton, Archbishop, 52.
Hamilton, David, 85.
Hamilton, Francis, 86.
Hamilton, James, 82.
Hamilton, James, Duke of, 42, 51.
Hamilton, John, 87.
Hamilton, Marquis of, 38.
Hay, Alexander, 1, 99.
Hay, James, of Fingask, 114.
Hay, Sir Alexander, 100.
Hay, Sir John, 87.
Henderson, Alexander, 6.
Hepburn, Sir Adam, 105.
Herries, Lord, 62.
Herries, Sir Hugh, 54.
Holderness, Earl of, 54.
Home, George, of Ford, 50.
Home, Sir George, 56, 57, 113.
Hope, Sir John, 5.
Hope, Sir Thomas, 109.
Huntington, Earl of, 56.
Huntly, George, Earl of, 38.
Huntly, Marquis of, 38.

Irving, Sir William, 50.

Jaffray, Alexander, 19.
Janson, William, 4.
Johnston, Arthur, 4, 47.
Justice Clerk, Office of, 29.
Justice-General, Office of, 28.
Johnston, Robert, 42.
Johnston, Sir Archibald, 102.

Kellie, Earls of, 47, 54.
Ker, Sir Robert, 89.
Ker, Sir William, 20, 89.
Kilpont, Lord, 119.
Kinghorn, Earl of, 55.
King's Advocate, Office of, 35.
Kinnoul, Earls of, 48.

Lanark, Earls of, 78, 89.
Law, Rev. Mungo, 5, 6.
Lawson, Richard, 103.
Lawson, Sir James, 105.
Lawson, Sir William, 103.
Lauderdale, Duke of, 44.
Lauderdale, Earl of, 44.
Leech, John, 4.

Lennox, Dukes of, 43, 117, 118.
Lennox, Earl of, 81, 84.
Leslie, General, 46, 74.
Lindsay, John, of Menmuir, 69.
Lindsay, Lord, 53.
Lord Clerk Register, Office of, 35.
Lothian, Earl of, 90—92.
Loudoun, Earl of, 51.

Macgill, James, 1.
Macgill, David, 108.
Maiden, Instrument of the, 37.
Maitland, Chancellor, 43, 69.
Maitland, Sir William, of Lethington, 67, 92.
Makgill, James, 53, 98.
Mar, Earls of, 59, 67.
Marischal, Office of, 31.
Marjoribanks, Thomas, 95.
Master of Requests, Office of, 33.
Maxwell, Lord, 60.
Melville, Andrew, 50.
Melville, James, 50.
Melville, Robert, Lord, 64.
Melville, Sir John, of Raith, 64.
Melville, Sir Robert, 64.
Melville, The Lords, 64.
Menteith, Earls of, 109, 119.
Menteith, Robert, 75.
Moncrieff, Sir John, 108.
Monk, General, 18.
Montrose, Earls of, 37, 45, 55.
Montrose, Marquis of, 38, 45, 46.
Morton, James, Earl of, 37.
Morton, William, Earl of, 60.
Murray, Earls of, 23, 38, 68.
Murray, Sir David, 113.
Murray, Sir Gideon, 42, 58, 65.
Murray, Sir William, 112.
Murrays of Tullibardine, 40.

Napier, Sir Archibald, 67.
Nicol, George, 62.
Nicolson, Sir Thomas, 110.
Norfolk, Lord, 68.
Norie, Professor Robert, 9.
Northumberland, Earl of, 37.

Ochiltree, Lord, 41, 42, 43.
Octavians, The, 43, 46, 71, 74.
Oliphant, Sir William, 109.
Overbury, Sir Thomas, 58.

Palatine, The Elector, 88.
Peckie, Lands of, 17.
Phillips, Edward, 20.
Pont, Rev. Timothy, 11.
Portland, Dukes of, 23.

INDEX.

Privy Seal, Office of, 34.

Rattray, Sir John, 39.
Richardson, Robert, 53.
Robertson, Patrick, 10.
Roxburgh, Earl of, 90, 94.
Ruthven, Lord, 153.

Sanquhar, Lord, 107.
Scot, David, of Allanhaugh, 1.
Scot, James, 96.
Scot, Professor Alexander, 9.
Scot, Robert, 1, 98.
Scot, Sir Alexander, 1.
Scot, Sir John, 1—24, 100, 121, 122.
Scotstarvet, 2, 20, 22.
Scott, David, of Scotstarvet, 2, 6, 22.
Scott, General John, 22, 23.
Scott, John, of Orchardfield, 1.
Scott, Robert, of Knightspottie, 1, 2.
Scott, Sir William, of Ardross, 1, 100.
Scott, Walter, of Lethan, 20.
Scott, William, 121.
Seaforth, Earl of, 47.
Secretary, Office of, 32.
Service Book, 5.
Seton, David, 113.

Seton, Lord, 44.
Skene, Sir John, 99.
Somerset, Earl of, 58.
Spottiswood, Archbishop, 49.
Spottiswood, Sir John, 50.
Spottiswood, Sir Robert, 50, 78.
Spang, Rev. William, 5.
Spence, Sir John, 107.
Spynie, Lord, 48.
St. Andrews, Colleges at, 2, 3, 6, 11.
St. Clair, Sir William, 51.
Steward, Office of, 30.
Stewart, Sir James, 42.
Stewart, Walter, of Blantyre, 55.
Stirling, Earl of, 75—77, 89.

Thirlestane, Lord, 43.
Traquair, Earl of, 60—64.
Treasurer, Office of, 33.

Walden, Lord, 57.
Wallace, Samuel, 13, 14.
Welsh, John, 50.
Wishart, Sir John, 111.
Wood, Andrew, of Largo, 112.
Wood, David, of Craig, 111.

www.ingramcontent.com/pod-product-compliance
Lightning Source LLC
Chambersburg PA
CBHW030347170426
43202CB00010B/1275